BIG BOOK
of Baby Knits

80+ Garment & Accessory Patterns

marie clai

Landauer Publishing

Landauer Publishing, www.landauerpub.com, is an imprint of
Fox Chapel Publishing Company, Inc.

Tricot bébé© 2010 by Editions Marie Claire Publishing - Société d'Information et
Créations (SIC)

© 2021 Fox Chapel Publishing Company, Inc., 903 Square Street, Mount Joy, PA 17552.

Big Book of Baby Knits is the English language edition of *Tricot bébé*, originally
published in French in 2010. This English edition published in 2021 by Fox Chapel
Publishing Company, Inc.

Project Team (English Edition)
Translator: Bonnie Gowans
Editor: Hayley DeBerard
Designer and Jacket Design: David Fisk
Proofreader: Nancy Arndt
Project Team (French Edition)
Editor: Thierry Lamarre
Coordination: Adeline Lobut
Layout: Charlotte Rion
Photographer: Pierre Nicou
Design: Frédérique Alexandre
Technical Explanation: Renée Méry
Charts and schematics: Olivier Ribaillier
Page design: Either Studio
Secrétariat de rédaction: Isabelle Misery
Cover design: Nicolas Valoteau
Phildar coordinators: Myriam Prez and Dilia
Lemaître
ISBN 978-1-947163-75-1

Library of Congress Control Number:
2021933672

We are always looking for talented
authors. To submit an idea,
please send a brief inquiry to
acquisitions@foxchapelpublishing.com.

Printed in Singapore
First Printing

About Marie Claire

Marie Claire's extensive range of best-selling books place an emphasis on taking care of yourself, having fun, understanding the world, and making life more beautiful. For 20 years, they've shown millions of readers the benefits of living in harmony with our environment, providing the keys to developing one's curiosity and passions, or preserving one's health. Marie Claire believes the printed "thing" has meaning and purpose, and they're dedicated to the satisfaction of their readers as they strive to inspire them through their impressive collection of titles.

BIG BOOK
of Baby Knits

80+ Garment & Accessory Patterns

Contents

Getting Started 8
  Gauge 8
  Choosing a Size 8
  Basic Stitches and Special Terms 8
  Abbreviations 8
  Hints and Tips 9
  Caring for Hand Knits 9

Hello Baby 12
  1 My First Cat 14
  2 Quiet Little Mouse 16
  3 Eyelet Edge Shawl Wrap 18

Sweet Treasures 20
  4 Keepsake Top 22
  5 Matching Keepsake Pants 23
  6 Basic Booties with Straps 24
  7 Baby's First Bonnet 25
  8 Thumbless Mittens 25

page 65

page 28

page 18

Baby Basics 26
  9 Sweetheart Hooded Jacket 28
  10 Busy Crawler Overalls 32
  11 Quick Garter Cap 33
  12 Lovebug Bunny 36
  13 Baby Love Pullover 38
  14 Baby Love Pants 40
  15 Little Lapin Slippers 41

Softness and Warmth 42
  16 Amour de Bébé Jumpsuit 44
  17 Simple Embellished Booties 47
  18 Chic Check Blanket 48
  19 Double-Breasted Striped Jacket 52

page 44

page 78

Little Flower 76

    32 Embellished Tunic Dress 78

    33 Embellished Leggings 80

Cute in Cables 82

    34 Braided Sprite Hat 86

    35 Braided Thumbless Mittens 86

    36 Seaside Cabled Sweater 87

    37 Seaside Cabled Bottoms 88

    38 Arctic Bear with Scarf 89

    39 Zip-Up Cabled Hooded Baby Bag 90

Snuggly and Warm 92

    40 X & O Hooded Jacket 94

    41 My First Scarf 98

    42 Simple Cap with Earflaps 99

    43 Tasseled Mittens 99

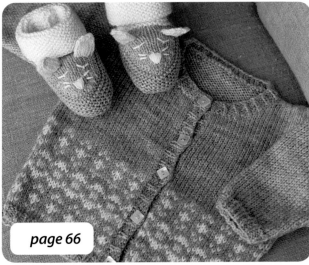

page 66

Classic Essentials 54

    20 Sleeveless Cocoon 56

    21 Long Sleeved Cocoon 58

    22 Cross Front Cardigan 62

    23 Soft-waist Wee Joggers 64

    24 Simple Buttoned Booties 65

    25 Mary Jane Style Booties 65

    26 Mouse Slippers 66

    27 Springtime Stranded Cardigan 66

    28 Sleepy Feline Friend 70

    29 Contrast Banded Cardigan 72

    30 Contrast Banded Bloomers 74

    31 Simple Knitted Baby Socks 75

page 87

page 94

page 102

Adorable Must-Makes 120

    53 Elvish Cabled Sack 122

    54 Pixie Hat 126

    55 Simple Wide Leg Pants 127

    56 Frog Button Coat 128

    57 Saddle Shoulder Pullover 132

    58 Little Rider Leggings 133

    59 Rocking Ribbed Romper 134

    60 Afternoon Slippers 135

    61 Scholar's Cardigan 138

    62 Scholar's Apprentice 140

    63 Artist's Tunic 143

Boutique Baby 144

    64 Lace Edge Bonnet 146

    65 Eyelet Wrap Front Cardigan 146

    66 Diamond Lace Blanket 150

    67 Eyelet Lace Cardi 151

    68 Simply Sweet Booties 153

    69 Daisy the Dormouse 154

    70 Too-Cute Tunic 158

    71 Baby Bell Bottoms 161

    72 Buttoned Baby Slippers 164

    73 Pretty Pocket Dress 165

page 110

Un-Bear-ably Cute 100

    44 Beary Sweet Cardigan 102

    45 Bear Paw Booties 104

    46 Grandpa Cardigan 105

    47 Little Man Pants 107

Nautical Newborns 108

    48 Classic Peacoat with Toggles 110

    49 Ocean Wave Socks 114

    50 Watch Cap 115

    51 Ocean Currents Sweater 116

    52 Button Front Sailor Pants 118

page 138

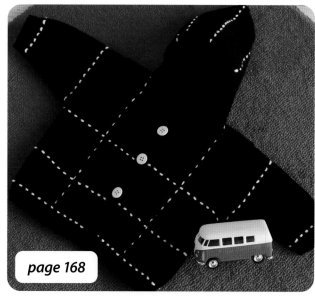

page 168

page 146

page 191

Bold and Beautiful Knits 166

74 Traveler Coat 168

75 Panda Pal 169

76 Sightseer Pullover 171

77 Trail Sweater 174

78 Simple Strappy Shoes 175

79 Voyager Booties 178

80 Journeyer's Pocket Dress 178

81 Busy Baby Bonet 182

82 Curiosity Cardigan 183

83 Sojourner Slacks 185

Floral and Fun 186

84 Carnation Cap 188

85 Chrysanthemum Cardigan 188

86 Pretty Picot Pants 190

87 Summery Slip-Ons 191

Index 192

Getting Started

Gauge

A **gauge swatch** is essential. It will let you knit an item to the right size. It should match the number of stitches and rows given for the pattern chosen. If you substitute yarns, check the gauge, and adjust your needle size as necessary.

If you have fewer stitches and rows, it means you are knitting too loosely and should go down in needle size.

If you have more stitches and rows, it means you are knitting too tightly and should go up in needle size.

Choosing a Size

Babies come in all shapes and sizes, and the measurements provided are only an approximate guide to use when selecting what pattern size to make. Size up if you are unsure about fit.

Some patterns have different **ages/sizes** listed. As a precaution, take your child's measurements before deciding on a size to knit in a given pattern.

Several sizes are given for each garment. To make it easier, we suggest you highlight the details that apply to the chosen size.

SIZE	WEIGHT	HEIGHT
Newborn	5½–7½ lbs (2.5 – 3.4 kg)	17½–21" (44.5 – 53.5 cm)
0 – 3 months	6½–12 lbs (2.9 – 5.4 kg)	20½–23" (52 – 58.5 cm)
3 – 6 months	12½–16 lbs (5.7 – 7.3 kg)	23½–26" (59.5 – 66 cm)
6 – 9 months	16½–19 lbs (7.5 – 8.6 kg)	26½–27½" (67.5 – 70 cm)
12 months	19½–22 lbs (8.8 – 10 kg)	28–29½" (71 – 75 cm)
18 months	22½–26 lbs (10.2 – 11.8 kg)	30–31½" (76 – 80 cm)
24 months	26½–30 lbs (12 – 13.6 kg)	32–33½" (81.5 – 80 cm)

Basic Stitches and Special Terms

1×1 Ribbing: Row 1: *Knit 1, purl 1 *. Repeat from *to*, ending with a knit 1. Row 2 and all subsequent rows: Work the stitches as they appear.

2×2 Ribbing: Row 1: *Knit 2, purl 2*. Repeat from *to* ending with knit 2. Row 2 and all subsequent rows: Work the stitches as they present.

2×1 Ribbing: *purl 2, knit 1.*

Edge stitch: The stitch at the beginning of each row. It can either be always knit or worked in stockinette.

Garter stitch: All the rows are knit stitches.

Reverse stockinette: Stockinette stitch worked on the wrong side.

Row: The stitches on one needle.

Skp: Slip 1, knit 1, pass slipped stitch over.

Slip: Pass the number of stitches indicated from the left to right needle purlwise without working them.

Stockinette stitch: Row 1: Knit. Row 2: Purl.

Take up: Place the stitches that were put on hold onto a needle to continue working on them. An example is when working the collar.

Yarn over: Bring the yarn over the right needle to make a loop. In certain patterns the yarn over will be dropped in the next row.

Abbreviations

CC: contrast color

dec: decrease

inc: increase

k: knit

k2tog: knit 2 stitches together (decrease)

MC: main color

p: purl

RS: right side

sl: slip

st(s): stitch(es)

St st: Stockinette stitch

WS: wrong side

YO: yarn over

Hints and tips

- **Avoid stopping working in the middle of a row:**
  This prevents having deformed stitches when you start
  working again or making a mistake when starting the stitch
  pattern again.

- **Knit several strands together:** If you do not want to work
  from several balls at once, prepare a ball with the number
  of strands needed to be held doubled. If you do this, just be
  careful you do not introduce loops when knitting and keep
  the tension on all the strands the same.

- **Safety:** When making the toys or softies, be sure to get
  gauge. The knitting should be tight and the seams solid to
  avoid the stuffing from coming out or being visible through
  the knitting.

Caring for Hand Knits

- For knits made using superwash wool, choose a wash setting
  with water around 85°F (30 °C) and use a gentle washing
  detergent or one designed for babies.

- Put small pieces, like socks and booties, in a laundry bag
  or pillowcase to avoid losing them or damaging them in
  the machine.

- To iron, use a damp, cotton pressing cloth between the
  knitting and the iron and press lightly. Never iron ribbing.

Projects

Hello Baby

1 - My First Cat

Yarn: DK weight (#3 Light)

Size: About 9" (22 cm) tall

Needle: Size US 2 (3 mm)

2 - Quiet Little Mouse

Yarn: DK weight (#3 Light)

Size: About 6" (15 cm) tall

Needle: Size US 2 (3 mm)

3 - Eyelet Edge Shawl Wrap

Yarn: DK weight (#3 Light)
Size: 29½ x 29½" (75 x 75 cm)
Needle: Size US 2 (3 mm)

1 - *My First Cat*

Worked from the toes to the top of the ears, this sweet little cat is an adorable softie for little ones to grasp and snuggle.

SIZE
- About 9" (22 cm) tall

YARN
- DK weight (#3 Light)
  Phildar Oxygène (40% acrylic, 35% chlorofiber, 25% combed wool; 148 yds [135 m]/1.76 oz [50 g]): Blanc (MC), and Lotus (CC), 1 skein each

NEEDLES
- Size US 2 (3 mm)
  Adjust needle size if necessary to obtain the correct gauge.

NOTIONS
- Fiber stuffing; tapestry needle

GAUGE
- 26 sts and 35 rows = 4" (10 cm) in St st

NOTES
- Body is worked in two flat pieces, starting at the bottom of the back leg and working up

Back

Legs
Cast on 5 sts in MC. Work in St st and inc 1 st at each end of Rows 1, 2, and 4. 11 sts. Work a total of 26 rows and put them on hold. Work a second leg same as first. At the end of the row 26, add 1 st then k the 11 sts in waiting.

Body
Continue in St st until row 40.

Arms
At the end of row 40, cast on 14 sts at each side for the arms. 51 sts. Inc at each side as follows:
2 sts once then 1 st twice. (3 inc rows). 59 sts.
On the row 50, dec at each end every row as follows:
Dec 1 st 2 times then 2 sts 1 time, then 14 sts 1 time.

Head
For the head continue working on the remaining 23 sts. On 7th head row (row 60), inc 1 st at each side. 25 sts.

Ears
On row 69, bind off the middle 3 sts and work the ears on either side separately changing to CC.
Dec 1 st at each side on row 5 and 7, then on each row until only 1 st remains. Put this piece on hold.

Front
Work as for the back.

Tail
Cast on 12 sts in MC. Work 4¾" (12 cm) in St st in MC then 1½" (4 cm) in CC. Cut the yarn leaving a tail and pull it through the sts tightly and secure the end. Sew the tail along the side.

Finishing
Pin the MC end of the tail between the back legs. Place the back and front RS together. Sew together leaving an opening under the arms for stuffing. Turn RS out and stuff. Seam the opening closed. Mark the neckline with a backstitch through all the thicknesses. Embroider claws, eyes, nose and whiskers with straight stitch in CC (see photo).

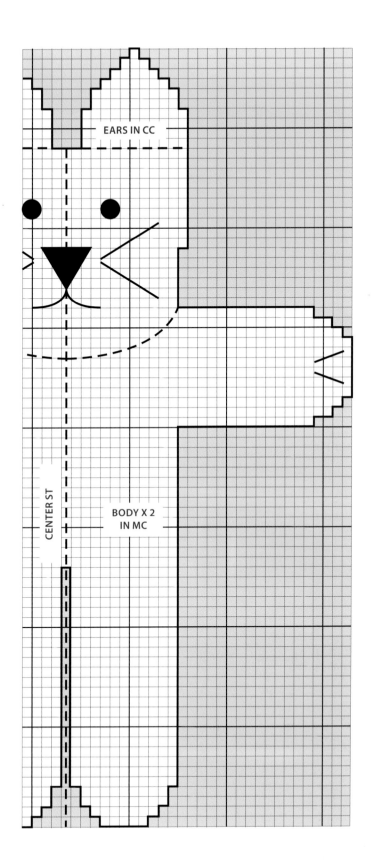

EARS IN CC

CENTER ST

BODY X 2
IN MC

2 - *Quiet Little Mouse*

Stitch a sweet friend or two for imaginative play. This cute little mouse is worked from the head down to the toes with the arms, ears, and tail attached once the body is completed.

SIZE
- About 6" (15 cm) tall

YARN
- DK weight (#3 Light)
  Phildar Oxygène (40% acrylic, 35% chlorofiber, 25% combed wool; 148 yds [135 m]/1.76 oz [50 g]): Blanc (MC), and Lotus (CC), 1 skein each

NEEDLES
- Size US 2 (3 mm)
  Adjust needle size if necessary to obtain the correct gauge.

NOTIONS
- Fiber stuffing; tapestry needle

GAUGE
- 26 sts and 35 rows = 4" (10 cm) in St st

Back
Start at the top of the head. Cast on 9 sts in MC and work in St st increasing at each side every other row as follows: 2 sts 2 times then 1 st 2 times, then 1 st 4 rows later. 23 sts. Work straight to row 40. On row 40, bind off the center 3 sts and then work the 10 sts left on each side separately for the legs. Dec 1 st at each edge on rows 49, 51, and 52. Bind off the remaining 4 sts.

Front
Work the same as the back.

Arms
Cast on 10 sts in MC. Work in St st decreasing 1 st on each side on rows 8, 10, and 11. Bind off the remaining 4 sts. Make 3 more arm pieces.

Ears
Cast on 13 sts in CC. Work in St st decreasing 1 st at each edge on row 13, 14, 15, and 15. Bind off the remaining 5 sts. Make 3 more.

Tail
Make a 6" (15 cm) cord using 5 strands of CC folded in half.

Finishing
Sew the ears and arms by placing them WS together. Add a bit of stuffing in the arms. Pin the ears and the arms to the body RS together. Sl the tail to the bottom of the body between 2 sts and knot the tail on the inside. Place the 2 body pieces RS together. Sew around leaving an opening under the arms.
Turn RS out, stuff and seam closed. Embroider the eyes, whiskers, and nose using CC.

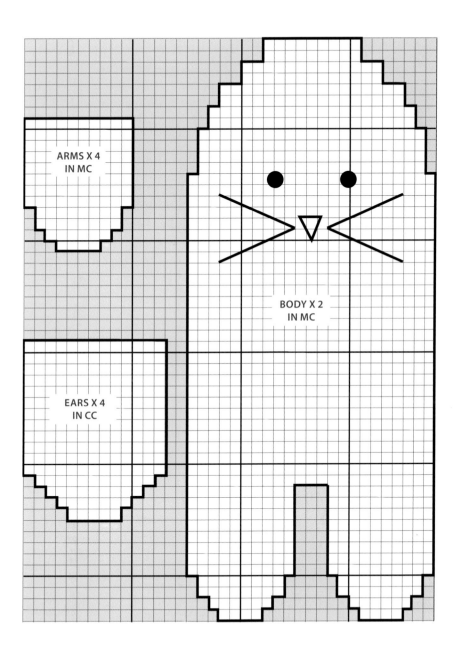

ARMS X 4
IN MC

EARS X 4
IN CC

BODY X 2
IN MC

3 - *Eyelet Edge Shawl Wrap*

Knit a special keepsake that will grow with baby through the years. This shawl can be used as a blanket during infant years and then wrapped over the shoulders for warmth as they grow.

SIZE
- 29½" x 29½" (75 x 75 cm)

YARN
- DK weight (#3 Light)
  Phildar Oxygène (40% acrylic, 35% chlorofiber, 25% combed wool; 148 yds [135 m]/1.76 oz [50 g]): Blanc, 7 skeins

NEEDLES
- Size US 2 (3 mm)
  Adjust needle size if necessary to obtain the correct gauge.

NOTIONS
- Size US D (3 mm) crochet hook

GAUGE
- 26 sts and 35 rows = 4" (10 cm) in St st

SPECIAL STITCHES
- **Single crochet:** sc
- **Chain stitch (crochet):** ch st
- **Crochet Picot:** *1 sc in each of the next 3 sts, ch 3. Repeat from *working the first sc in the same st as the last sc worked.

Shawl
Cast on 198 sts. Work in St st. Starting on row 13, work following the chart to make 2 horizontal rows of eyelets then work 2 vertical rows of eyelets with 10 St sts at each side and the center worked in St st between the eyelets. After 40 eyelets along the outer vertical rows, work 2 new horizontal rows of eyelets, reversing the pattern of the first set. End with 12 rows of St st. Bind off the border.

Crochet Border
Work a row of sc all around the shawl, then a row of picot.

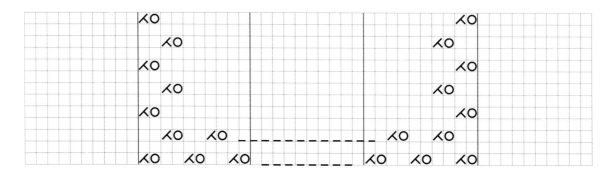

K ON RS, P ON WS

YO

K2TOG

4 - Keepsake Top

Yarn: Fingering weight (#1 Super Fine)

Sizes: Newborn (3 months, 6 months)

Needles: Size US 1 (2.5 mm) and Size US 2 (3 mm)

5 - Matching Keepsake Pants

Yarn: Fingering weight (#1 Super Fine)

Sizes: Newborn (3 months, 6 months)

Needles: Size US 0 (2 mm) and Size US 1 (2.5 mm)

Sweet Treasures

6 – Basic Booties with Straps

Yarn: Fingering weight (#1 Super Fine)
Size: Newborn to 3 months
Needles: Size US 1 (2.5 mm)

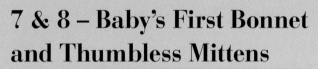

7 & 8 – Baby's First Bonnet and Thumbless Mittens

Yarn: Fingering weight (#1 Super Fine)
Sizes: 3 months (6 months)
Needles: Size US 2 (3 mm)

4 - *Keepsake Top*

Make a cherished heirloom with a matching layette set. The top is worked in pieces and seamed before being tied with the belt. The back is worked in two pieces that overlap to close.

SIZES
- Newborn (3 months, 6 months)

YARN
- Fingering weight (#1 Super Fine)
  Phildar Super Baby (70% acrylic, 30% wool; 117 yds [107 m]/0.88 oz [25 g]): Cygne, 3 (4, 4) skeins

NEEDLES
- Size US 1 (2.5 mm) and Size US 2 (3 mm)
  Adjust needle size if necessary to obtain the correct gauge.

NOTIONS
- Two garment snaps; tapestry needle

GAUGE
- 30 sts and 40 rows = 4" (10 cm) in St st using larger needle

SPECIAL STITCHES
- **Sleeve dec s (RS only):** Dec 2 sts in from the side
- **To dec 1 st at each side:** K 2, double dec, work across to the last 4 sts k2tog, k2
- **To dec 2 sts at each side:** K2, SKPO, work to the last 5 sts, k3tog, k2
- **SKPO:** Sl 1, k 1, pass slipped st over.
  Double dec: Sl 1, k2tog, pass the slipped st over.

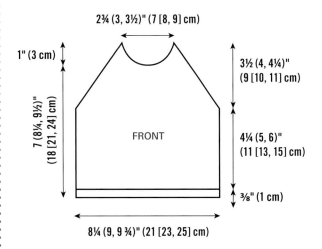

2¾ (3, 3½)" (7 [8, 9] cm)

1" (3 cm)

3½ (4, 4¼)" (9 [10, 11] cm)

7 (8¼, 9½)" (18 [21, 24] cm)

FRONT

4¼ (5, 6)" (11 [13, 15] cm)

⅜" (1 cm)

8¼ (9, 9 ¾)" (21 [23, 25] cm)

Front
Cast on 62 (68, 74) sts using smaller needles. Work 8 rows in garter st. Change to larger needles and continue in St st. At 4¾ (5½, 6¼)" (12 [14, 16] cm) above the Cast on edge, work the 2 sts at each side in garter st decreasing at each side (*see Special Stitches*) every other row as follows: dec 2 sts 2 times then dec 1 st 16 times to shape the armhole. **AT THE SAME TIME**, at 7 (8¼, 9½)" (18 [21, 24] cm) from the cast on edge, bind off the center 12 (14, 16) sts and work each side separately. Bind off 2 sts once then 1 st once at the neckline then the remaining 2 sts.

Left Half Back
Cast on 40 (44, 48) sts on smaller needles. Work 8 rows in garter st. Change to larger needles and continue in St st. At 4¾ (5½, 6¼)" (12 [14,16] cm) above the cast on edge, work the sleeve shaping on the left side as for the front. At 8¼ (9½, 10½)" (21 [24, 27] cm) above the cast on edge, bind off the remaining 20 (22, 24) sts. Work right half back reversing the shaping.

Sleeves
Cast on 42 (46, 50) sts on smaller needles. Work 8 rows in garter st. Change to larger needles and work in St st, increasing 1 st at each side as follows: every 6 rows 6 times (every 7 rows 7 times, every 8 rows 8 times). 54 (60, 66) sts. At 4¼ (5½, 6)" (11 [14, 15] cm) above the cast on edge, work the 2 sts at either side in garter st and dec at 2 sts in from the edge, every other row as follows: 1 st 18 times (2 sts 1 time then 1 st 19 times, 2 sts 2 times then 1 st 20 times). At 7¾ (9½, 10¼)" (20 [24, 26] cm) above the cast on edge bind off the remaining 18 sts.

Belts
Cast on 4 sts on larger needles and work 11¾ (13¾, 13¾)" (30 [35, 35] cm) in garter st and bind off. Make 2.

Finishing
Sew the armholes. Sew the underarm seam on the sleeves then sew the side seams leaving a ¾" (2 cm) opening on the left side for the belt at 1 (1½, 2)" (3 [4, 5] cm) below the armhole.
Neckline Border: Pick up 62 (68, 74) sts with smaller needles around the neckline. Work 3 rows in garter st and bind off.
Back Borders: Pick up 62 (72, 82) sts with smaller needles at the edge of each half back. Work 3 rows in garter st.
Sew the belts to the back at the height of the opening. Sew snaps at the neckline to keep the back closed.

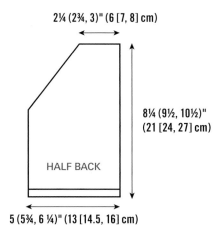

2¼ (2¾, 3)" (6 [7, 8] cm)

8¼ (9½, 10½)" (21 [24, 27] cm)

HALF BACK

5 (5¾, 6 ¼)" (13 [14.5, 16] cm)

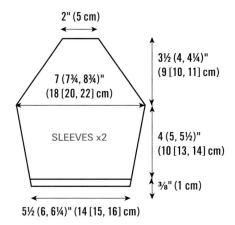

2" (5 cm)

3½ (4, 4¼)" (9 [10, 11] cm)

7 (7¾, 8¾)" (18 [20, 22] cm)

SLEEVES x2

4 (5, 5½)" (10 [13, 14] cm)

⅜" (1 cm)

5½ (6, 6¼)" (14 [15, 16] cm)

5 - Matching Keepsake Pants

The perfect pairing to the top, these pants act as a diaper cover and allow for easy leg movement.

SIZES

- Newborn (3 months, 6 months)

YARN

- Fingering weight (#1 Super Fine) Phildar Super Baby (70% acrylic, 30% wool; 117 yds [107 m]/0.88 oz [25 g]): Cygne, 2 (3, 4) skeins

NEEDLES

- Size US 0 (2 mm) and Size US 1 (2.5 mm) *Adjust needle size if necessary to obtain the correct gauge.*

NOTIONS

- Elastic thread; tapestry needle

GAUGE

- 33 sts and 61 rows = 4" (10 cm) in garter st using larger needle

NOTES

- The pants are worked in one piece starting at front waistband

---

Pants

Cast on 64 (68, 74) sts on smaller needles. Work ¾" (2 cm) of 1 x 1 ribbing. Change to larger needles and working in garter st, work 10 incs evenly on row 1. 74 (78, 84) sts. At 4 (4¼, 4 ½)" (10 [10.5, 11.5] cm) from the beginning divide the work. On the 23 (25, 28) RS sts, dec 1 st 1 time for all sizes. Then dec 1 st every 6 rows 4 times, 1 st every 4 rows 2 times, then every 2 rows: dec 1 st 4 times then 2 sts 6 times. (1 st every 6 rows 4 times, 1 st every 4 rows 3 times, then every 2 rows: dec 1 st 3 times then 2 sts 7 times, 1 st every 6 rows 4 times, 1 st every 4 rows 3 times, then every 2 rows: dec 1 st 4 times and 2 sts 8 times. *Note: Put on hold when there are 6 sts remaining.*

Work the leftmost 23(25, 28) sts, dec as for the RS with the dec worked on the left edge.

5 - *Matching Keepsake Pants* (continued)

Pick up the 28 center sts and work straight for 3 (3¼, 3½)" (8 [8.5, 9] cm) then working on all the sts (40) continue dec 2 sts every 2 rows 3 times at the edges. 28 sts.

On the back, inc at each side as follows: every 2 rows inc 2 sts 6 times, 1 st 5 times, then 1 st every 4 rows 2 times, then 1 st every 6 rows 4 times (every 2 rows inc 2 sts 7 times, 1 st 4 times, then 1 st every 4 rows 3 times, 1 st every 6 rows 4 times , every 2 rows inc 2 sts 8 times, 1 st 5 times, then 1 st every 4 rows 3 times and then 1 st every 6 rows 4 times). 74 (78, 84) sts.

At 14¼ (15, 16)" (36 [38, 41] cm) long, evenly dec 10 sts. 64 (68, 74) sts.

Switch to smaller needles, work ¾" (2 cm) of 1 x 1 ribbing then bind off.

Leg Borders

Cast on 61 (65, 69) sts on smaller needles. Work 6" (15 cm) in garter st. Bind off loosely.

Finishing

Sew the sides. Sew the edges of the leg border together in round. Pass several rows of elastic thread under the ribbing at the waist.

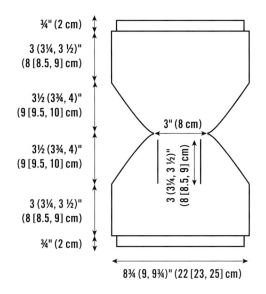

¾" (2 cm)

3 (3¼, 3 ½)" (8 [8.5, 9] cm)

3½ (3¾, 4)" (9 [9.5, 10] cm)

3" (8 cm)

3½ (3¾, 4)" (9 [9.5, 10] cm)

3 (3¼, 3 ½)" (8 [8.5, 9] cm)

3 (3¼, 3 ½)" (8 [8.5, 9] cm)

¾" (2 cm)

8¾ (9, 9¾)" (22 [23, 25] cm)

6 - *Basic Booties with Straps*

SIZE
• Newborn

YARN
• Fingering weight (#1 Super Fine) Phildar Super Baby (70% acrylic, 30% wool; 117 yds [107 m]/0.88 oz [25 g]): Cygne, 1 skein

NEEDLES
• Size US 1 (2.5 mm)

NOTIONS
• Two buttons; tapestry needle

NOTES
• The booties are worked in one piece starting at the middle of the sole

Booties

Cast on 41 sts in garter st increasing 1 st each edge and at each side of the center 3 sts every 2 rows 4 times. 57 sts.

Work 10 rows in garter st to make the sides. Break the yarn.

To make the top of the foot, sl 22 sts, work 1 x 1 ribbing on the center 13 sts joining each side of this piece to the sides by k together the last st of each row with the 1st st in waiting for a total of 11 times.

Work 1 x 1 ribbing on the remaining 35 sts for 2¼" (6 cm) and bind off. Fold the bootie and seam the back, reversing the seam on the last 1" (3 cm).

Strap

Cast on 15 sts. Work 15 rows in garter st and bind off.

Sew the strap at the edge along the top of the side. Place a button at the other side to fix the strap. Be sure to reverse the attachment on the other bootie.

7 - Baby's First Bonnet

8 - Thumbless Mittens

Complete this matching layette set with a simple bonnet and mittens.

SIZES
- 3 months (6 months)

YARN
- Fingering weight (#1 Super Fine)
  Phildar Super Baby (70% acrylic, 30% wool; 117 yds
  [107 m]/0.88 oz [25 g]): Cygne, 1 skein

NEEDLES
- Size US 2 (3 mm)

NOTIONS
- Cable needle; tapestry needle

Bonnet

Cast on 106 (114) sts. Work 1" (2.5 cm) in garter st then change
to St st. At 3¼ (4)" (8.5 [10] cm), work crown shaping as follows:
1 edge st, *k 20 (22) sts, put 3 sts on the cable needle and place
in back, then k together the 1st st of each needle, then 2nd st
of each needle and the 3rd st of each needle (3 dec) * 4 times, 1
edge st.
Repeat this dec row working 3 less sts between the dec, every
4 rows 2 more times, then every 2 rows 4 (5) times. 22 (18) sts.
Cut the yarn leaving a long tail for seaming and pass it through
the remaining sts. Pull tight, secure the tail and seam the
bonnet closed.

SIZES
- 3 months (6 months)

YARN
- Fingering weight (#1 Super Fine)
  Phildar Super Baby (70% acrylic, 30% wool; 117 yds
  [107 m]/0.88 oz [25 g]): Cygne, 1 skein

NEEDLES
- Size US 2 (3 mm)

NOTIONS
- Tapestry needle

Mittens

Cast on 18 (21) sts. Work 1" (2.5 cm) in garter st then continue
in St st and inc 1 st each side on row 2 and 6. 22 (25) sts.
At 3 (3½)" (8 [9] cm), dec 1 st at each side once, then after
working 4 rows straight, dec 2 st at each side every 2 rows 2
times. Bind off the remaining sts.
Work the other half and seam with RS together.

Baby Basics

9 – Sweetheart Hooded Jacket

Yarn: Bulky weight (#5 Bulky)
Sizes: 3 months (6 months, 12 months)
Needles: Size US 7 (4.25 mm)

9 - *Sweetheart Hooded Jacket*

This cuddly hooded jacket is must-have basic in every baby's wardrobe. The sleeves can be rolled to allow for easy movement of hands and the hood will keep your baby warm on the coolest days.

SIZES
- 3 months (6 months, 12 months)

YARN
- Bulky weight (#5 Bulky)
  Phildar Partner 6 (50% polyamide, 25% wool, 25% acrylic; 71 yds [65 m]/1.76 oz [50 g]): Blanc, 8 (9, 10) skeins

NEEDLES
- Size US 7 (4.5 mm)
  Adjust needle size if necessary to obtain the correct gauge.

NOTIONS
- Four buttons; stitch makers; tapestry needle

GAUGE
- 17 sts and 36 rows = 4" (10 cm) in garter st

Back
Cast on 46 (50, 54) sts. Work in garter st.
At 8¼ (9, 9¾)" (21 [23, 25] cm), start raglan shaping by binding off 2 sts at each side then dec 2 sts in from each side as follows:
3 months: dec 1 st every 2 rows 17 times and then 1 st after 4 rows.
6 months: 1 st every 2 rows 17 times then 1 st every 4 rows 2 times.
12 months: 1 st every 2 rows 17 times then 1 st every 4 rows 3 times.
At 12½ (13¾, 15)" (32 [35, 38] cm), bind off the remaining 6 (8. 10) sts.

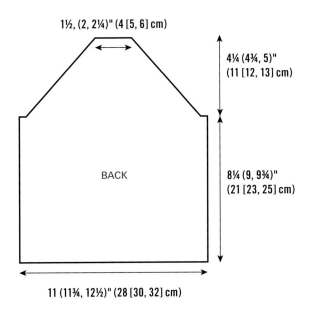

1½, (2, 2¼)" (4 [5, 6] cm)

4¼ (4¾, 5)" (11 [12, 13] cm)

BACK

8¼ (9, 9¾)" (21 [23, 25] cm)

11 (11¾, 12½)" (28 [30, 32] cm)

Right Front

Cast on 30 (32, 34) sts. Work in garter st.

At 6¼ (7, 7½)" (16 [18, 19] cm), make a set of two 1 st buttonholes—the first, 2 sts in from the edge and the 2nd 5 (6, 7) sts from the first. Work another set of buttonholes 4 (4¼, 4¾)" (10 [11. 12] cm) higher.

AT THE SAME TIME, at 8¼ (9, 9¾)" (21 [23, 25] cm), work the armhole shaping along the left side as for the back.

At 11 (12¼, 13)" (28 [31, 33] cm), shape the neckline by binding off 4 (5, 6) sts then 3 sts, then 2 sts, then 1 st.

Left Front

Work as for the right front reversing shaping and do not work the buttonholes.

Sleeves

Cast on 24 (26, 28) sts. Work in garter st and inc 1 st at each side every 5 rows 9 (10, 11) times. 42 (46, 50) sts.

At 5 (6, 7)" (13 [15, 18] cm), shape the raglan as follows:

3 months: bind off 2 sts at each side 1 time, then 1 st every 2 rows 13 times, then 1 st every 4 rows 3 times.

6 months: bind off 2 sts at each side 1 time, then 1 st every 2 rows 15 times, then every 4 rows 3 times.

12 months: bind off 2 sts at each side 1 time, then 1 st every 2 rows 18 times, then 1 st every 4 rows 2 times.

When 9½ (10½, 12¼)" (24 [27, 31] cm) long, bind off all 6 sts.

Hood

Cast on 28 (30, 34) sts. Work garter st and inc 1 st along the right edge every 14 rows 4 times. 32 (34, 38) sts. Put marker A at the edge at 6¼ (6¾, 7)" (16 [17, 18] cm), marker B at 7¾ (8¼, 8¾)" (20 [21, 22] cm), then marker C 1½" (4 cm) above. At 7¾ (8¼, 8¾)" (20 [21. 22] cm), you have reached the middle of the hood. Work the other half reversing the directions.

Finishing

Seam the armholes and sides and sleeve seams. Fold the hood along the center line, matching markers A and C. Seam the back from the bottom to markers A/C. Flatten the top to bring B over A/C and work a horizontal seam. Bind off 1½" (4 cm) at the right edge of the hood, sew the necklines together leaving 1" (3 cm) free on each front. Sew on buttons.

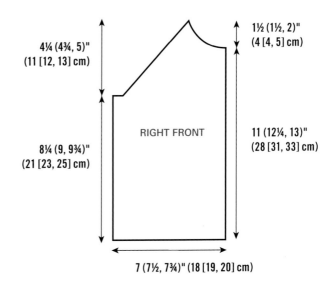

4¼ (4¾, 5)" (11 [12, 13] cm)

1½ (1½, 2)" (4 [4, 5] cm)

RIGHT FRONT

8¼ (9, 9¾)" (21 [23, 25] cm)

11 (12¼, 13)" (28 [31, 33] cm)

7 (7½, 7¾)" (18 [19, 20] cm)

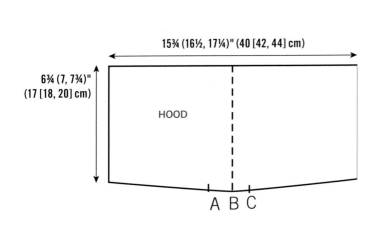

15¾ (16½, 17¼)" (40 [42, 44] cm)

6¾ (7, 7¾)" (17 [18, 20] cm)

HOOD

A B C

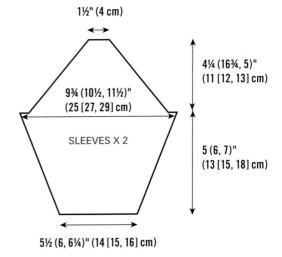

1½" (4 cm)

4¼ (16¾, 5)" (11 [12, 13] cm)

9¾ (10½, 11½)" (25 [27, 29] cm)

SLEEVES X 2

5 (6, 7)" (13 [15, 18] cm)

5½ (6, 6¼)" (14 [15, 16] cm)

10 – Busy Crawler Overalls

Yarn: Fingering weight (#1 Super Fine)

Sizes: 3 months (6 months, 12 months)

Needles: Size US 2 (3 mm)

11 – Quick Garter Cap

Yarn: Bulky weight (#5 Bulky)
Sizes: 6 months (12 months)
Needles: Size US 7 (4.5 mm)

10 - *Busy Crawler Overalls*

Active babies need garments that move with them. These classic overalls let baby easily crawl without wiggling out of them.

SIZES
- 3 months (6 months, 12 months)

YARN
- Fingering weight (#1 Super Fine)
  Phildar Super Baby (70% acrylic, 30% wool; 117 yds
  [107 m]/0.88 oz [25 g]): Cygne, 4 (4, 5) skeins

NEEDLES
- Size US 2 (3 mm)
  Adjust needle size if necessary to obtain the correct gauge.

NOTIONS
- Two buttons; tapestry needle

GAUGE
- 25 sts and 54 rows = 4" (10 cm) in garter st

NOTES
- Overalls are worked in two pieces and seamed, starting with the bottom of the left leg

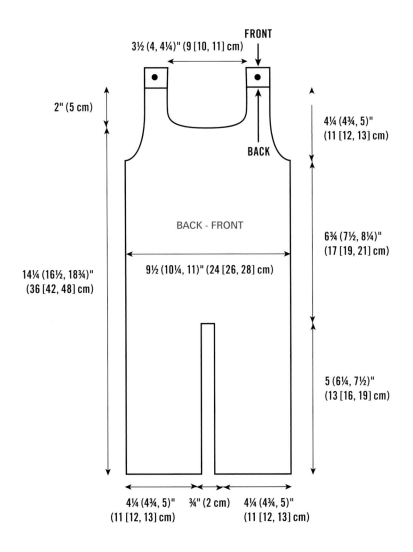

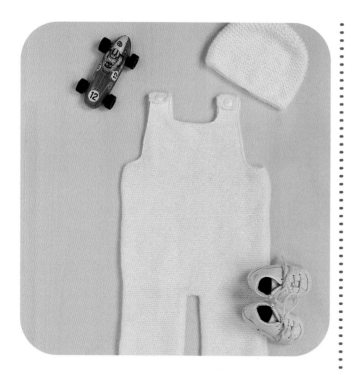

11 - *Quick Garter Cap*

Stitch a quick and easy garter hat with bulky yarn for extra warmth.

SIZES
- 6 months (12 months)

YARN
- Bulky weight (#5 Bulky)
  Phildar Partner 6 (50% polyamide, 25% wool, 25% acrylic; 71 yds [65 m]/1.76 oz [50 g]): Blanc, 1 skein

NEEDLES
- Size US 7 (4.5 mm)
  Adjust needle size if necessary to obtain the correct gauge.

NOTIONS
- Tapestry needle

GAUGE
- 17 sts and 36 rows = 4" (10 cm) in garter st

Bonnet

Cast on 51 (58) sts. Work in garter st.
At 3 (4)" (8 [10] cm), start decreasing for the crown as follows: 1 edge st, *k2tog, k 5 (6) sts* 7 times, 1 edge st.
Repeat these decs one over the other every 2 rows 5 (6) more times.
Cut the yarn leaving a tail for seaming. Pull through the remaining sts and seam the bonnet with fine sts.

Back

Cast on 27 (30, 33) sts. Work in garter st. When 5 (6¼, 7½)" (13 [16, 19] cm) long put the sts on hold. Work a right leg the same.
Cast on 6 sts for the crotch then k the sts from the left leg. 60 (66, 72) sts. Continue in garter st.
At 11¾ (13¾, 15¾)" (30 [35, 40] cm), start the armhole shaping by binding off at each side every 2 rows as follows: 6 sts 1 time, 4 sts 1 time, 2 sts 1 time and 1 st 3 times. 30 (36, 42) sts.
At 14¼ (16½, 18¾)" (36 [42, 48] cm), bind off the center 6 (8, 10) sts. Finish each side separately by binding off every 2 rows along the neckline as follows: 3 sts 1 time, 2 sts 1 time and 1 st 2 times.
At 16 (18½ 20¾)" (41 [47, 53] cm) bind off the remaining 5 (7, 9) sts.

Front

Work the same as the back but working longer straps.
When 16½ (18¾, 21¼)" (42 [48, 54] cm) long, make a 1 st buttonhole in the center of each strap.
When 17 (19¼, 21¾)" (43 [49, 55] cm) long, bind off the remaining 5 (7, 9) sts.

Finishing

Sew the sides. Sew the inner leg seam.
Borders: From the WS pick up and k the number of sts indicated for each size and bind off as they are formed.
Armholes: 88 (94, 100) sts, front neckline 58 (60, 62) sts, back neckline 46 (48, 50) sts.
Sew a button on the back straps.

12 – Lovebug Bunny

Yarn: Sport weight (#2 Fine)
Size: About 15¾" (40 cm) tall
Needles: Size US 8 (5 mm)

13 & 14 – Baby Love Pullover and Pants

Yarn: Sport weight (#2 Fine)
Sizes: 3 months (6 months, 12 months)
Needles: Size US 8 (5 mm)

15 – Little Lapin Slippers

Yarn: Sport weight (#2 Fine)
Size: 3 to 6 months
Needles: Size US 2 (3 mm)

12 - *Lovebug Bunny*

Give your baby somebunny to love with this long-legged hare in need of a hug!

SIZE
• About 15¾" (40 cm) tall

YARN
• Sport weight (#2 Fine)
Phildar Pilou (50% acrylic, 13% wool, 29% polyamide, 8% spandex; 66 yds [60 m]/0.88 oz [25 g]): Blanc (MC), 2 skeins; Galet (CC1), 1 skein
Phildar Lambswool (51% wool, 49% acrylic; 147 yds [134 m]/1.76 oz [50 g]): Dragée (CC2), 1 skein

NEEDLES
• Size US 8 (5 mm)
Adjust needle size if necessary to obtain the correct gauge.

NOTIONS
• Black embroidery thread; synthetic stuffing; tapestry needle

GAUGE
• 24 sts and 38 rows = 4" (10 cm) in St st in MC
Take into account the elasticity of the yarn and let the swatch rest several hours before measuring

NOTES
• The heart is worked in duplicate stitch on the front
• Duplicate each st as shown on chart
• Rabbit is worked in one piece starting with the bottom of the right foot
• Rabbit's pullover is worked in one piece starting with the front hem

Back
Cast on 11 sts in MC. Work in St st. At 5¾" (14.5 cm), inc 1 st at the right edge. At 6" (15 cm) put on hold. Work the left leg but inc at the left edge. At 6" (15 cm) work across then cast on 2 sts for the crotch and then work across the sts on hold. 26 sts. At 9½" (24 cm), bind off 7 sts at each side for the shoulders. 12 sts. Work the head following the chart.

Front
Work as for the back but do not make the ears.

Arm
Cast on 16 sts in MC. Work 4¾" (12 cm) in St st and bind off. Make one more arm same as first.

Finishing
Place the back and front RS together and seam around leaving an opening and leaving the ears free inside. Turn inside out and stuff with filling. Seam closed. Seam the edges of the arms and pleat the bound off row. Sew the arms to each side of the body. With a piece of MC encircle the feet 1½" (4 cm) from the bottom, the arms 1" (3 cm) from the end and at the base of the ears. Knot tightly. Embroider the muzzle with CC2 and the eyes in black embroidery thread with straight st.

Mini Pullover
Cast on 33 sts in CC1 and work in St st. At 1" (3 cm), cast on 10 sts at each end for the sleeves. 53 sts. At 2¼" (6 cm), bind off the 13 center sts for the neckline and cast on 13 sts on the next row. When 4¾" (12 cm) long, bind off all 33 sts. Embroider a heart using CC2 and chart in the middle of front. Seam the top of the arms and sides.

HEAD CHART

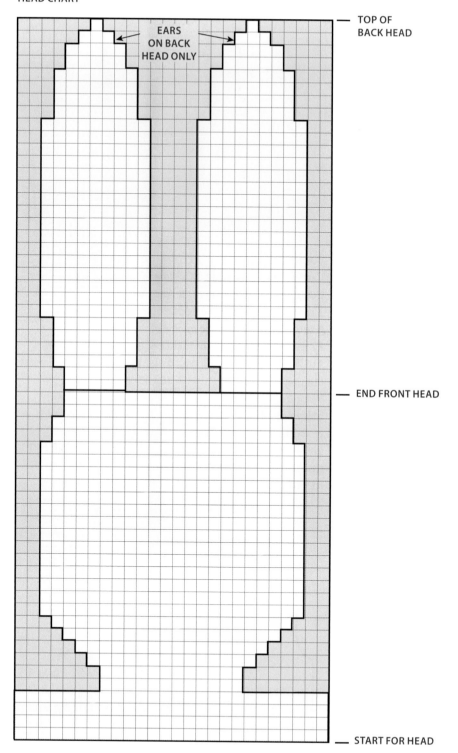

EARS ON BACK HEAD ONLY

— TOP OF BACK HEAD

— END FRONT HEAD

— START FOR HEAD

HEART EMBROIDERY CHART

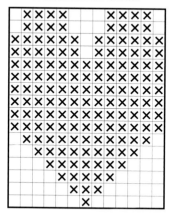

☒ = CC2 worked into Rabbit Pullover in duplicate st

13 - *Baby Love Pullover*

Show your love of your child with French flair. The Baby Love Pullover features embroidered words and a duplicate stitch heart for visual interest.

SIZES
- 3 months (6 months, 12 months)

YARN
- Sport weight (#2 Fine)
  Phildar Pilou (50% acrylic, 13% wool, 29% polyamide, 8% spandex; 66 yds [60 m]/0.88 oz [25 g]):
  Galet (MC), 3 (4, 5) skeins
  Phildar Lambswool (51% wool, 49% acrylic; 147 yds [134 m]/1.76 oz [50 g]): Dragée (CC1), Blanc (CC2), 1 skein each

NEEDLES
- Size US 8 (5 mm)
  Adjust needle size if necessary to obtain the correct gauge.

NOTIONS
- Three garment snaps; tapestry needle

GAUGE
- 24 sts and 38 rows = 4" (10 cm) in St st in MC
  Take into account the elasticity of the yarn and let the swatch rest several hours before measuring

NOTES
- The heart is worked in duplicate stitch on top of the knitting following the motif
- The letters are embroidered with chain stitch

Back
Cast on 54 (62, 66) sts in MC. Work ¾" (2 cm) of 2 x 2 ribbing. Continue in St st working as follows:

3 months: inc 1 st in the middle of the first row. 55 sts.

6 months: dec 1 st in the middle of the first row. 61 sts.

12 months: inc 1 st in the middle of the first row = 67 sts.

At 5½ (6¼, 7)" (14 [16, 18] cm), divide the work in 2 equal parts binding off the center stitch. 27 (30, 33) sts each side. Work each side separately. Next row start the armholes as follows: bind off 2 sts every 2 rows 2 times then 1 st every 2 rows 2 times. 21 (24, 27) sts. At 9½ (10½, 11¾)" (24 [27, 30] cm) long, shape the neckline by binding off 7 (8, 9) sts then 4 sts 1 time. At 9¾ (11, 12¼)" (25 [28, 31] cm), bind off all 10 (12, 14) shoulder sts.

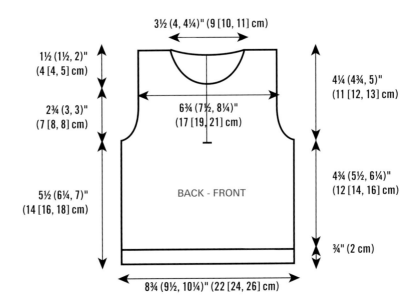

1½ (1½, 2)" (4 [4, 5] cm)

2¾ (3, 3)" (7 [8, 8] cm)

5½ (6¼, 7)" (14 [16, 18] cm)

3½ (4, 4¼)" (9 [10, 11] cm)

6¾ (7½, 8¼)" (17 [19, 21] cm)

4¼ (4¾, 5)" (11 [12, 13] cm)

4¾ (5½, 6¼)" (12 [14, 16] cm)

¾" (2 cm)

BACK - FRONT

8¾ (9½, 10¼)" (22 [24, 26] cm)

Front

Work the front as for the back without forming the opening. At 8¾ (9½, 10¼)" (22 [24, 26] cm), bind off the center 7 (9, 11) sts and work each side separately. Bind off at the neckline every 2 rows as follows: 3 sts 1 time, 2 sts 1 time, 1 st 2 times then work 4 rows and bind off 1 st. At 9¾ (11, 12¼)" (25 [28, 31] cm) bind off all the remaining 10 (12, 14) shoulder sts.

Sleeves

Cast on 38 (42, 46) st with MC. Work ¾" (2 cm) of 2 x 2 ribbing. Continue in St st working 1 dec in the middle of the first row then increasing at each side as follows: 1 st every 5 rows 8 times. 53 (59, 65) sts. At 5½ (6¼, 7½)" (14 [16, 19] cm) long, bind off every 2 rows, 1 st 2 times then 2 sts 2 times. Bind off the remaining sts.

Finishing

Embroider in cross-stitch in CC2 on the 3rd row of St sts on the body and the sleeves placing the first st in the middle of the work and the others spaced 2 sts apart. Enlarge the photocopy to the size indicated. Trace the embroidery motif on tracing paper and baste to the front. Embroider the letters in chain stitch in CC2. Gently remove the tissue paper. Embroider the heart in duplicate st using CC1 following the chart. Sew the shoulders.

Neckline Border: Pick up and k 68 (72, 76) sts in MC around the neckline. Work ¾" (2 cm) of 2 x 2 ribbing and bind off loosely.

Back Opening Border: Pick up and k 40 sts in MC on each side of the back opening. Work 3 rows of 2 x 2 ribbing and bind off. Cross then sew the 2 edges to the middle of the back. Sew on snaps to close the back.

Sleeves: Seam the sleeves to the armhole and seam the sleeve seam and side seam.

HEART CROSS-STITCH CHART

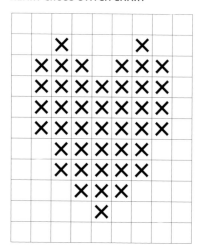

 = Duplicate st in CC1

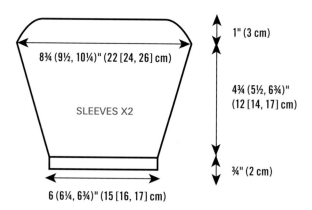

¾" (2 cm)

5½" (14 cm)

¾" (2 am)

6¼" (16 cm)

1" (3 cm)

8¾ (9½, 10¼)" (22 [24, 26] cm)

4¾ (5½, 6¾)" (12 [14, 17] cm)

SLEEVES X2

¾" (2 cm)

6 (6¼, 6¾)" (15 [16, 17] cm)

14 - *Baby Love Pants*

Designed to coordinate perfectly with the Baby Love Pullover, these soft waist pants will keep your child cozy and comfortable.

SIZES

- 3 months (6 months, 12 months)

YARN

- Sport weight (#2 Fine)
  Phildar Pilou (50% acrylic, 13% wool, 29% polyamide, 8% spandex; 66 yds [60 m]/0.88 oz [25 g]):
  Galet (MC), 3 (4, 5) skeins
  Phildar Lambswool (51% wool, 49% acrylic; 147 yds [134 m]/1.76 oz [50 g]): Blanc (CC), 1 skein

NEEDLES

- Size US 8 (5 mm)
  Adjust needle size if necessary to obtain the correct gauge.

NOTIONS

- Elastic thread for waist; tapestry needle

GAUGE

- 24 sts and 38 rows = 4" (10 cm) in St st in MC
  Take into account the elasticity of the yarn and let the swatch rest several hours before measuring

NOTES

- Pants are worked in one piece starting with the bottom of the left leg

Back

Cast on 28 (31, 34) sts in MC. Work in St st. Inc at the right edge as follows: inc 1 st every 6 (5, 8) rows 9 times. 37 (40, 43) sts At 6 (7, 8¼)" (15 [18, 21] cm) put the sts on hold and work the right leg increasing at the left edge. Then take up the sts on hold and continue working on the 74 (80, 86) sts dec 1 st each side of the center 2 sts every row 3 times then every other row 3 times. 62 (68, 74) sts. At 11½ (13¼, 15¼)" (29.5 [34, 38.5] cm), work 1" (3 cm) of 1 x 1 ribbing and bind off.

Front

Work the same as the back.

Finishing

Sew the sides.
Lower leg borders: Pick up and k 58 (62, 66) sts in MC along the bottom of each leg. Work ¾" (2 cm) of 2 x 2 ribbing and bind off. Seam the inner leg seams. Embroider a line of cross st in CC on the 3rd row of St with each st covering 1 st and 2 rows. Place the first st in the middle of the front and the remaining spaced 2 sts apart. Thread several rows of elastic thread through the waist ribbing.

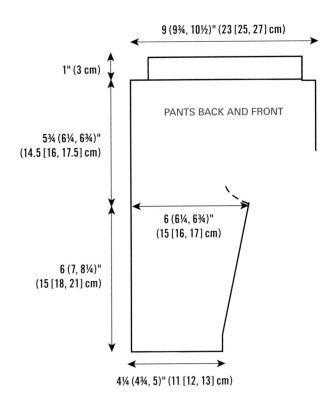

9 (9¾, 10½)" (23 [25, 27] cm)

1" (3 cm)

PANTS BACK AND FRONT

5¾ (6¼, 6¾)" (14.5 [16, 17.5] cm)

6 (6¼, 6¾)" (15 [16, 17] cm)

6 (7, 8¼)" (15 [18, 21] cm)

4¼ (4¾, 5)" (11 [12, 13] cm)

15 - *Little Lapin Slippers*

Baby will love grabbing their feet with these fun bunny slippers. These are not recommended for babies who can walk as the bottoms do not have traction.

SIZE
- 3 to 6 months

YARN
- Sport weight (#2 Fine)
Phildar Lambswool (51% wool, 49% acrylic; 147 yds [134 m]/1.76 oz [50 g]): Blanc (MC), 1 skein
Phildar Pilou (50% acrylic, 13% wool, 29% polyamide, 8% spandex; 66 yds [60 m]/0.88 oz [25 g]): Galet (CC), 1 skein

NEEDLES
- Size US 2 (3 mm)
Adjust needle size if necessary to obtain the correct gauge.

NOTIONS
- Black embroidery thread; tapestry needle

GAUGE
- 26 sts and 36 rows = 4" (10 cm) in St st in MC
Take into account the elasticity of the yarn and let the swatch rest several hours before measuring

Sole
Cast on 7 sts in MC. Work in St st. Inc 1 st on each side of row 1, 2, 4, and 6. Then dec 1 st at each side of rows 26, 28, 30, 32. Bind off the remaining 7 sts.

Side and Foot
Cast on 36 sts in CC. Work in reverse St st as follows: 6 rows CC, 17 rows MC then work in St st.
On row 11, put the 12 sts at each side on hold. To work the top of the foot, continue working on the 12 center sts. Dec 1 st at each side on row 12, 14, 16, and 17.
Put the remaining 4 sts on hold. Take up the right 12 sts on hold and pick up and k 14 sts along the edge of the top, then the 4 sts at the end of the foot, then pick up and k 14 sts along the other side and then the 12 sts on hold on the left. 56 sts.

Cuff
Work 10 rows of St st then 4 rows in reverse St st in CC. Bind off loosely.

Ears
Cast on 10 sts in MC. Work in St st decreasing 1 st at each side of row 16, 18, and 19. Bind off the remaining 4 sts. Work a second piece the same then 2 more worked in CC but in reverse St st.

Finishing
Seam the cuff and the back reversing the seam on the reverse St st at the start of the cuff. Sew around the sole then form a welt just above the sole by seaming together the first and last row of CC.
Sew a MC ear and a CC ear RS together leaving the bottom open. Turn inside out and place the edge of the ears towards the center near the cuff as shown. Sew them on the slipper. Embroider the eyes and nose with straight stitch with black embroidery thread.

16 – Amour de Bébé Jumpsuit

Yarn: Sport weight (#2 Fine)

Sizes: 3 months (6 months, 12 months)

Needles: Size US 8 (5 mm)

17 – Simple Embellished Booties

Yarn: Sport weight (#2 Fine)

Size: 3 to 6 months

Needles: Size US 8 (5 mm)

Softness and Warmth

18 – Chic Check Blanket

Yarn: Sport weight (#2 Fine)
Size: 23½ x 33¾" (60 x 86 cm)
Needles: Size US 6 (4 mm)

16 - *Amour de Bébé Jumpsuit*

Dress your little one in love with this classic jumpsuit with a twist. The French phase, Amour de Bébé, is embroidered with chain stitch and accented with a duplicate stitch heart.

SIZES
- 3 months (6 months, 12 months)

YARN
- Sport weight (#2 Fine)
  Phildar Pilou (50% acrylic, 13% wool, 29% polyamide, 8% spandex; 66 yds [60 m]/0.88 oz [25 g]):
  Blanc (MC), 6 (7, 8) skeins
  Phildar Lambswool (51% wool, 49% acrylic; 147 yds [134 m]/1.76 oz [50 g]): Flanelle (CC1), Dragée (CC2), 1 skein each

NEEDLES
- Size US 8 (5 mm)
  Adjust needle size if necessary to obtain the correct gauge.

NOTIONS
- Size US G-6 (4 mm) crochet hook; seven white buttons; three garment snaps; tapestry needle

GAUGE
- 24 sts and 38 rows = 4" (10 cm) in St st in MC
  Take into account the elasticity of the yarn and let the swatch rest several hours before measuring

NOTES
- The letters are embroidered in chain stitch
- Onesie is worked in two pieces and seamed, starting with the lower back left leg

SPECIAL STITCHES
- **Single crochet:** sc
- **Chain stitch (crochet):** ch st
- **Crochet Picot:** *1 sc in each of the next 3 sts, ch 3. Repeat from *working the first sc in the same st as the last sc worked.

Back

Cast on 28 (31, 34) sts in MC. Work in St st, inc 1 st at the right edge every 9 (11, 13) rows 5 times. At 4¾ (6, 7)" (12 [15, 18] cm) put the 33 (36, 39) sts on hold. Work the right leg working the inc at the left edge. At 4¾ (6, 7)" (12 [15, 18] cm), cast on 1 st for the crotch then work the left leg sts. Work straight on 67 (73, 79) sts until it is 13¼ (15¼, 17¼)" (34 [39, 44] cm) long. Bind off the center st in the back to create an opening and work each side separately. Bind off for the armhole shaping every 2 rows as follows: 2 sts once then 1 st 3 times. 26 (29, 32) sts. At 17¼ (19¾, 22)" (44 [50, 56] cm), shape the neckline by binding off every 2 rows: 7 (8, 9) sts then 4 sts. At 17¾ (20, 22½)" (45 [51, 57] cm), bind off the remaining 15 (17, 19) shoulder sts.

Front

Work as for the back without making the opening. At 13¼ (15¼, 17¼)" (34 [39, 44] cm), bind off at each side, every 2 rows as follows: 2 sts 2 times and 1 st 3 times = 53 (59, 65) sts. At 16 (18½, 20½)" (41 [47, 52] cm), bind off the center 7 (9, 11) sts and work each side separately. Shape the neckline by binding off every 2 rows as follows: 3 sts 1 times, 2 sts 1 time and 1 st 3 times.

At 17¾ (20, 22½)" (45 [51, 57] cm), bind off all 15 (17, 19) shoulder sts.

Sleeves

Cast on 38 (42, 46) sts. Work ⅝" (1.5 cm) of 2 x 2 ribbing then continue in St st. Inc 1 st at each side as follows:

3 months: every 4 rows 10 times. 58 sts.

6 months: every 4 rows 11 times. 64 sts.

12 months: every 5 rows 12 times. 70 sts.

At 5 (5¾, 7¼)" (12.5 [14.5, 18.5] cm) long, bind off at each side every 2 rows as follows: 1 st 3 times, 2 sts 2 times then the remaining sts.

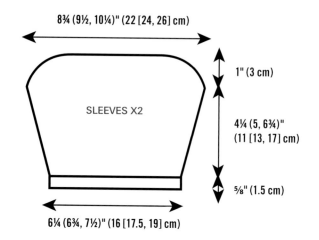

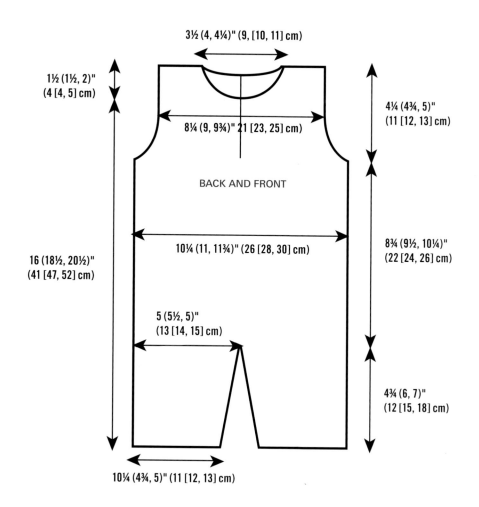

16 - *Amour de Bébé Jumpsuit* (continued)

Finishing

Enlarge the motif to the size indicated and trace on tracing paper and baste to the front. Mark the edge of the heart with a basting stitch. Embroider the text in chain stitch using CC1. Remove the paper gently and fill in the heart with duplicate stitch in CC2. Sew the shoulders.

Neckline Border: Pick up and k 68 (72, 76) sts in MC around the neckline. Work ⅝" (1.5 cm) of 2 x 2 ribbing starting and ending with k3. Bind off.

Back Opening Borders: pick up and k 40 (44, 48) sts on each side of the opening. Work 4 rows of 2 x 2 ribbing and bind off. Overlap and sew the 2 border ends to the middle of the back. Finish the border with a row of picots.

Seam the sleeves to the armhole, then seam the side seams and sleeves. Pick up and k 60 (64, 68) sts at the bottom of each leg and work ⅜" (1 cm) of 2 x 2 ribbing starting and ending with k3. Bind off.

Inner Leg Button Bands: Pick up and k 92 (108, 124) sts along the back inner leg. Work ⅝" (1.5 cm) of 2 x 2 ribbing starting and ending with 1 edge st. Repeat on the front working 7 buttonholes in the center section as follows: the first at 3 (4, 4) sts in from the side and the remaining spaced every 13, alternating 15 (16, 18) sts apart.

Sew the buttons on the back band. Sew the snaps to close the back.

5½" (14 cm)

¾" (2 am)

6¼" (16 cm)

¾" (2 cm)

HEART STITCH CHART

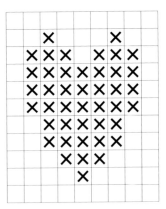

x   Duplicate st in CC2

17 - *Simple Embellished Booties*

Basic booties look extra special with simple embellishments. In this design, add a duplicate stitch heart to match the Amour de Bebe Jumpsuit.

SIZE
- 3 to 6 months

YARN
- Sport weight (#2 Fine)
  Phildar Pilou (50% acrylic, 13% wool, 29% polyamide, 8% spandex; 66 yds [60 m]/0.88 oz [25 g]): Blanc (MC), 1 skein
  Phildar Lambswool (51% wool, 49% acrylic; 147 yds [134 m]/1.76 oz [50 g]): Dragée (CC), 1 skein

NEEDLES
- Size US 8 (5 mm)
  Adjust needle size if necessary to obtain the correct gauge.

NOTIONS
- Tapestry needle

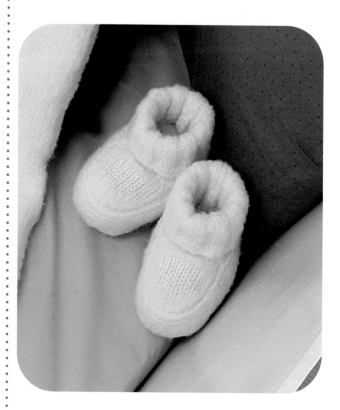

GAUGE
- 24 sts and 38 rows = 4" (10 cm) in St st in MC
  Take into account the elasticity of the yarn and let the swatch rest several hours before measuring

Booties

Cast on 11 sts for the heel of the sole. Work in garter st. At 3" (8 cm) long, add 24 sts at each end to make the side of the bootie. Work the first row as follows: 23 st, k2tog, 9 st, k2tog, and 23 st. 57 st. Bind off at 4½" (11.5 cm) long.

Cast on 42 sts for the leg. Work 2¾" (7 cm) of 2 x 2 ribbing and bind off. Cast on 12 st for the top of the foot. Work in St st. Dec first st in from the edge at each side on rows 13, 15, 17 and 18. Bind off the remaining 4 sts.

Finishing

Embroider a heart in the center of each top in CC. Close the heel by bringing together the edges of the cuff. Sew around the sole. Sew in the top opposite the heel. Seam the cuff, sides, and the top.

**BOOTIES HEART
CROSS-STITCH CHART**

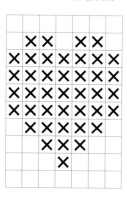

| x | Duplicate st in CC2 |

18 - *Chic Checked Blanket*

Knit a beautiful nursery blanket using intarsia for a unique checked look. Change the colors to suit any decor.

SIZE
- 23½ x 33¾" (60 x 86 cm)

YARN
- Sport weight (#2 Fine)
  Phildar Pilou (50% acrylic, 13% wool, 29% polyamide, 8% spandex; 66 yds [60 m]/0.88 oz [25 g]):
  Blanc (C1), 7 skeins; Galet (C2), 4 skeins; Poudre (C3) 6 skeins

NEEDLES
- Size US 8 (5 mm)
  Adjust needle size if necessary to obtain the correct gauge.

NOTIONS
- Tapestry needle

GAUGE
- 24 sts and 38 rows = 4" (10 cm) in St st in MC
  Take into account the elasticity of the yarn and let the swatch rest several hours before measuring

NOTES
- Blanket squares are worked in intarsia using 1 ball for each square
- Be sure to cross the yarns when changing colors

Blanket

Cast on 136 sts in C1. Work 3 rows in garter st then change to St st and work as follows: 34 sts C1, 34 sts in C3, 34 sts C1, 34 sts C3. Change the colors every 54 rows following the chart. Work 3 rows in garter in C1. Bind off. Pick up and k 255 sts in C1 at each side. Work 3 rows in garter st and bind off.

BLANKET INTARSIA CHART

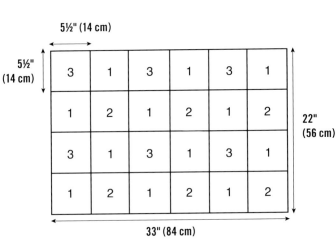

5½" (14 cm)

5½" (14 cm)

22" (56 cm)

33" (84 cm)

Knit direction

1 = C1
2 = C2
3 = C3

19 – Double-Breasted Striped Jacket

Yarn: Sport weight (#2 Fine)

Sizes: 3 months (6 months, 12 months)

Needles: Size US 8 (5 mm)

19 - *Double-Breasted Striped Jacket*

Dapper and darling, this knitted jacket is stylishly adorned with decorative double-breasted buttons.

SIZES

- 3 months (6 months, 12 months)

YARN

- Sport weight (#2 Fine)
  Phildar Pilou (50% acrylic, 13% wool, 29% polyamide, 8% spandex; 66 yds [60 m]/0.88 oz [25 g]):
  Galet (MC), 5 (6, 7) skeins; Blanc (CC), 2 skeins

NEEDLES

- Size US 8 (5 mm)
  Adjust needle size if necessary to obtain the correct gauge.

NOTIONS

- Six white buttons; tapestry needle

GAUGE

- 24 sts and 38 rows = 4" (10 cm) in St st in MC
  Take into account the elasticity of the yarn and let the swatch rest several hours before measuring

Back

Cast on 64 (70, 76) sts in MC in St st.
At 6¾ (7½, 8 ¼)" (17 [19, 21] cm), work 2" (5 cm) in MC then change to CC. At 7 (7¾, 8¾)" (18 [20, 22] cm), shape the armholes by binding off 3 sts at each side then then dec 1 st every row 6 times, then dec 1 st every other row 16 (18, 20) times. At 11 (12¼, 13¼)" (28 [31, 34] cm), bind off the remaining 14 (16, 18) sts.

Right Front

Cast on 42 (45, 48) sts in MC. Work in St st as for the back. At 5½ (6, 6 ¼)" (14 [15, 16] cm) long, make two 1 st buttonholes, the first 3 sts from the edge of the middle front, the 2nd, 8 (9, 10) sts after the first. Make 2 other sets of 2 buttonholes at 7¾ (8½, 9¼)" (19.5 [21.5, 23.5] cm) (in the middle of the white band) then at 9¾ (11, 12¼)" (25 [28, 31] cm).
AT THE SAME TIME, at 7 (7¾, 8¾)" (18 [20, 22] cm), shape the armhole by binding off 3 sts at the left side, then dec 1 st every row 6 times then 1 st every 2 rows 14 (16, 18) times.
At 9¾ (11, 12¼)" (25 [28, 31] cm) long, shape the neckline by binding off along the right edge every other row as follows:
3 months: 6 sts, 5 sts, 4 sts, then 2 st.
6 months: 6 sts 2 times, 4 sts, 2 sts.
12 months: 7 sts, 6 sts, 4 sts, and 2 sts.
Bind off the remaining 2 sts.

Left Front

Work the same reversing shaping and omitting the buttonholes.

Left Sleeve

Cast on 37 (41, 45) sts in MC. Work in St st. Inc 1 st at each side as follows:

3 months: Every 5 rows 8 times. 52 sts.
6 months: Every 5 rows 9 times. 59 sts.
12 months: Every 6 rows 10 times. 65 sts.
AT THE SAME TIME, at 4 (4¼, 6¼)" (10 [11,16] cm), work 2" (5 cm) in CC then change to MC. At 4¼ (4¾, 6¾)" (11 [12, 17] cm), shape the armholes: bind off 3 sts at each side then dec 1 st every row 6 times. Dec 1 st every 2 rows as follows: 1 st 16 times at the right edge and 1 st at the left edge 14 (16, 18) times. After the armhole dec are worked, bind off at the left side to shape the neckline every 2 rows as follows: 4 st 1 time, 3sts 1 time, then 2 sts.

Right Sleeve

As for the left sleeve reversing shaping.

Hood

Cast on 31 (34, 37) sts in MC. Work in St st. Inc 1 st at the RS every 6 rows 7 times. 38 (41, 44) sts. At 10½ (11½, 13)" (27 [29, 33] cm), dec 1 st at the RS every 6 rows 7 times. At 15 (15¾, 17¼)" (38 [40, 44] cm) bind off all 31 (34, 37) sts.

Finishing

Hood Border: Pick up and k 111 (117, 123) sts in CC along the straight edge of hood. Work 4 rows of 1 x 1 ribbing then bind off.
Assemble Jacket: Sew the back then the front sleeves. Fold the hood and sew the back seam. Seam to the neckline with the edges meeting at the front edges. Sew on buttons.

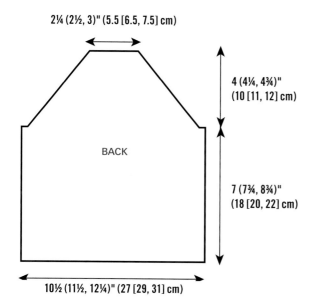

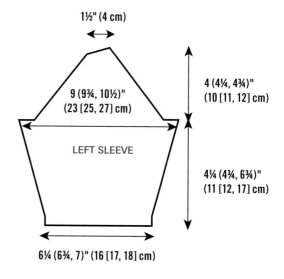

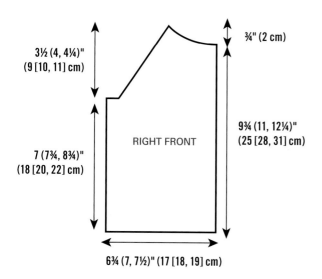

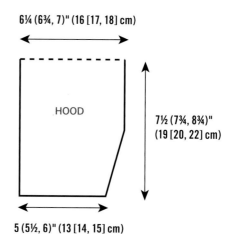

Classic Essentials

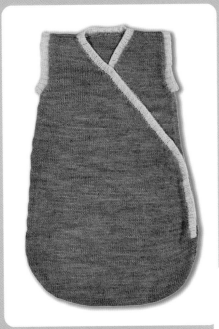

20 – Sleeveless Cocoon

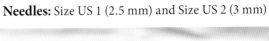

Yarn: Sport weight (#2 Fine)

Size: Newborn to 3 months

Needles: Size US 1 (2.5 mm) and Size US 2 (3 mm)

21 – Long Sleeved Cocoon

Yarn: Sport weight (#2 Fine)

Size: Newborn to 3 months

Needles: Size US 1 (2.5 mm) and Size US 2 (3 mm)

20 - *Sleeveless Cocoon*

Keep baby warm in their first few months with a cocoon of lambswool. This classic baby garment allows for legs to move and kick while keeping the core extra warm.

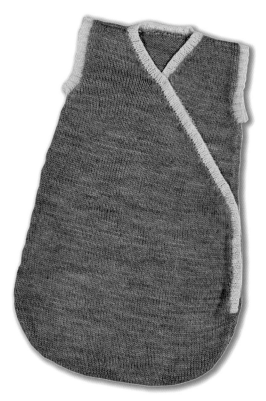

SIZE
- Newborn to 3 months

YARN
- Sport weight (#2 Fine)
  Phildar Lambswool (51% wool, 49% acrylic; 147 yds [134 m]/1.76 oz [50 g]): Flanelle (MC), 4 skeins; Blanc (CC), 1 skein

NEEDLES
- Size US 1 (2.5 mm) and Size US 2 (3 mm)
  Adjust needle size if necessary to obtain the correct gauge.

NOTIONS
- Six garment snaps; tapestry needle

GAUGE
- 26 sts and 36 rows = 4" (10 cm) in St st using larger needles

Back

Cast on 32 sts in MC using larger needles. Work in St s. Inc every 2 rows at each side as follows: 6 sts once, 5 sts once, 4 sts once, 3 sts once, 2 sts once, 1 st 7 times, then inc 1 st after 4 rows and then after 6 rows. 90 sts.

At 5½" (14 cm), dec 1 st each side, every 10 rows 9 times. 72 sts.

At 15" (38 cm), shape the armholes: bind off at each side every 2 rows as follows: 2 sts 2 times then 1 st 3 times. 58 sts.

At 18¾" (48 cm), bind off the center 16 sts. Work each side separately shaping the neckline by working 2 rows then bind off 5 sts.

At 19¼" (49 cm) long, bind off the 16 shoulder sts.

Right front

Cast on 32 sts in MC, using larger needles. Work in St st. Inc every 2 rows at each side as follows: 6 sts once, 5 sts once, 4 sts once, 3 sts once, 2 sts once, 1 st 7 times then inc 1 st after 4 rows then after 6 rows. 90 sts.

Continue shaping the left edge as for the back (side, armhole, and shoulder) but along the right edge: At 4¼" (11 cm), bind off the first 3 sts then dec 1 st every 20 rows 3 times.

At 11" (28 cm), shape the diagonal edge by binding off every 2 rows as follows: (1 st once, then 2 sts once) 14 times then 1 st 10 times.

Left Front

Cast on 2 sts in MC using larger needles. Work in St st. At the right edge: Dec 1 st every 10 rows 3 times then at 4" (10 cm), bind off the armhole as for the back. At 8¼" (21 cm), bind off the 16 shoulder sts.

At the left edge: Inc *1 st after 2 rows, 1 st in the next row* 10 times then inc 1 st every row 17 times. At 5½" (14 cm), shape the diagonal edge for the neckline by binding off every 2 rows as follows: 1 st once, 2 sts once and then 1 st 10 times.

Finishing

Right Front Border: Starting with the 3 bound off sts, pick up and k 124 sts up to the shoulder in CC using smaller needles. Work ¾" (2 cm) of 2 x 2 ribbing starting and ending with k3. Bind off.

Back Neckline Border: Pick up and k 32 sts in CC with smaller needles along the back neckline. Work ¾" (2 cm) of 2 x 2 ribbing starting and ending with k3. Bind off. Sew the shoulders.

Armhole Borders: Pick up and k 74 sts in CC with smaller needles around each armhole. Work ¾" (2 cm) of 2 x 2 ribbing and bind off.

Sew the bottom 4" (10 cm) of the left front to the back. Place a marker at the back edge, 4¼" (11 cm) from the cast on edge.

Left Border: Starting at the shoulder, pick up and k 30 sts in CC using smaller needles along the diagonal edge of the neckline. Then pick up and k 94 sts along the front edge and the back to the marker. Work ¾" (2 cm) of 2 x 2 rib starting and ending with k2.

Place the right front and back RS together and sew the side and bottom to the 3 bound off sts.

Use snaps between the 2 fronts to keep them shut.

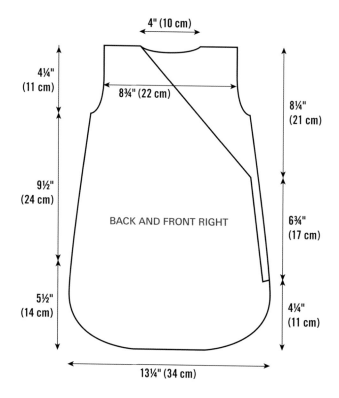

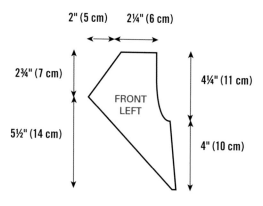

21 - *Long Sleeved Cocoon*

Like its sleeveless counterpart, the Long Sleeved Cocoon is designed for warmth.
Adding sleeves provides an extra layer of wool to keep baby cozy.

SIZE
- Newborn to 3 months

YARN
- Sport weight (#2 Fine)
  Phildar Lambswool (51% wool, 49% acrylic; 147 yds
  [134 m]/1.76 oz [50 g]): Dragée (MC), 5 skeins; Flanelle
  (CC), 1 skein

NEEDLES
- Size US 1 (2.5 mm) Size US 2 (3 mm)
  *Adjust needle size if necessary to obtain the
  correct gauge.*

NOTIONS
- Six garment snaps; three gray satin bows (optional);
  tapestry needle

GAUGE
- 26 sts and 36 rows = 4" (10 cm) in St st using
  larger needles

Back
Cast on 32 sts in MC, on larger needles. Work in St st. Inc every
2 rows as follows: 6 sts, 5 sts, 4 sts, 2 sts, 2 sts, 1 st 7 times, then
work 4 rows and inc 1 st and work 6 rows and inc 1 st. 90 sts.
At 5½" (14 cm), dec 1 st each side every 10 rows 9 times. 72 sts.
At 15" (38 cm), shape the armholes: bind off at each side every
other row as follows: 2 sts 2 times and 1 st 3 times. 58 sts.
At 18¾" (48 cm), bind off the center 16 sts and then work each
side separately. Work 2 rows and bind off 5 sts at the neckline.
At 19¼" (49 cm), bind off the remaining 16 shoulder sts.

Right front
Cast on 32 sts in MC on larger needles. Work in St st. Inc every
2 rows as follows: 6 sts, 5 sts, 4 sts, 3 sts, 2 sts each 1 time, then
1 st 7 times, then work 4 rows, inc 1 st 1 time then work 6 rows
and inc 1 st 1 time. 90 sts.
Continue working the left edge as for the back (to shape side,
armhole, and shoulder) but on the right edge: at 4¼" (11 cm),
bind off 3 sts then dec 1 st every 20 rows 3 times.
At 11" (28 cm), shape the diagonal edge by binding off every 2
rows as follows: (1 st 1 time, then 2 sts 1 time) 14 times then 1 st
10 times.

Left Front
Cast on 2 sts in MC on larger needles. Work in St st. Work the
right and left edges differently as follows: At the right edge: dec
1 st every 10 rows 3 times. At 4" (10 cm), bind off the armhole
as for the back and at 8¼" (21 cm) bind off the remaining 16
shoulder sts.
At the left edge: Inc *1 st after 2 rows, 1 st on next row * 10 times
then 1 st every row 17 times.
At 5½" (14 cm), shape the diagonal neckline by binding off every
2 rows at the left edge as follows: 1 st 1 time, 2 sts 1 time, and 1
st 10 times.

Sleeves

Cast on 44 sts in CC, on smaller needles. Work ⅝" (1.5 cm) 2 x 2 ribbing. Change to larger needles and work in St st with MC or CC. Inc at each side: every 5 rows 6 times then every 4 rows 2 times. 60 sts.

At 5" (12.5 cm), bind off at each side every other row as follows: 2 sts 2 times and 3 sts 1 time. Bind off remaining sts.

Finishing

Right Front Border: Starting at the 3 bound off sts, pick up and k 124 sts up to the shoulder in CC on smaller needles. Work ¾" (2 cm) of 2 x 2 ribbing starting and ending with k3. Bind off.
Back Neckline Border: Pick up and k 32 sts along the back neckline in CC on smaller needles. Work ¾" (2 cm) of 2 x 2 ribbing starting and ending with k3. Bind off. Sew the left shoulder. Sew the bottom 4" (10 cm) on the left front to the back. Place a marker at 4¼" (11 cm) from the beginning.
Left Border: Starting at the shoulder, pick up and k 30 sts in CC on smaller needles along the diagonal edge of the neckline then 94 sts along the front and back edges up to the marker. Work ¾" (2 cm) of 2 x 2 ribbing starting and ending with k 2. Place the right front RS together against the back and sew the right shoulder, side and bottom up to the 3 bound off sts. Seam the sleeves and seam to the armholes. Keep fronts closed with snaps between them. Sew bows on the border.

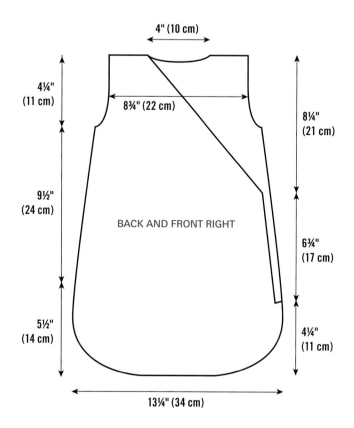

4" (10 cm)

4¼" (11 cm)

8¾" (22 cm)

8¼" (21 cm)

9½" (24 cm)

BACK AND FRONT RIGHT

6¾" (17 cm)

5½" (14 cm)

4¼" (11 cm)

13¼" (34 cm)

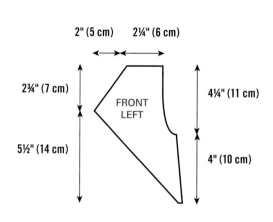

2" (5 cm)   2¼" (6 cm)

2¾" (7 cm)

FRONT LEFT

4¼" (11 cm)

5½" (14 cm)

4" (10 cm)

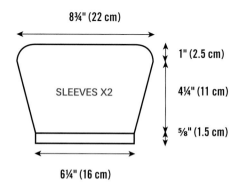

8¾" (22 cm)

1" (2.5 cm)

SLEEVES X2

4¼" (11 cm)

⅝" (1.5 cm)

6¼" (16 cm)

22 – Cross Front Cardigan

Yarn: Sport weight (#2 Fine)
Sizes: Newborn (3 months, 6 months)
Needles: Size US 1 (2.5 mm) and Size US 2 (3 mm)

23 – Soft-waist Wee Joggers

Yarn: Sport weight (#2 Fine)
Sizes: Newborn (3 months, 6 months)
Needles: Size US 1 (2.5 mm) and Size US 2 (3 mm)

24 – Simple Buttoned Booties

Yarn: Sport weight (#2 Fine)
Size: Newborn to 3 months
Needles: Size US 2 (3 mm)

25 – Mary Jane Style Booties

Yarn: Fingering weight (#1 Super Fine)
Size: Newborn to 3 months
Needles: Size US 1 (2.5 mm)

26 – Mouse Slippers

Yarn: Sport weight (#2 Fine)
Size: Newborn to 3 months
Needles: Size US 1 (2.5 mm) and Size US 2 (3 mm)

27 – Springtime Stranded Cardigan

Yarn: Sport weight (#2 Fine)
Sizes: Newborn (3 months, 6 months)
Needles: Size US 1 (2.5 mm) and Size US 2 (3 mm)

22 - *Cross Front Cardigan*

This baby basic is an essential for cooler weather. The simple design is easy to slip on when the temperature falls and just as easy to take off when the day warms up.

SIZES

- Newborn (3 months, 6 months)

YARN

- Sport weight (#2 Fine)
  Phildar Lambswool (51% wool, 49% acrylic; 147 yds [134 m]/1.76 oz [50 g]): Dragée or Flanelle, 3 (3, 4) skeins

NEEDLES

- Size US 1 (2.5 mm) and Size US 2 (3 mm)
  Adjust needle size if necessary to obtain the correct gauge.

NOTIONS

- Cable needle; three garment snaps; tapestry needle

GAUGE

- 26 sts and 36 rows = 4" (10 cm) in St st using larger needles

SPECIAL STITCHES

- **Front neckline dec s are made on the RS 1 st in from the edge.** To dec 2 sts work as follow on the right front: k 1, place 2 st on cable needle and hold in back. K together the first st on each needle then k together the second st on each needle. Work as follows for the left front: work to the last 5 sts, place the next 2 sts on cable needle and hold in front. K together the first st on each needle then the second st on each needle, k 1.
  To dec 1 st on the right front: k1, k2tog. On the left front work to the last 3 sts, sl 1, k 1 pass slipped st over, k1.

Back

Cast on 57 (63, 69) sts on larger needles. Work ⅜" (1 cm) garter st, then change to St st.
At 4¾" (5½, 6¼)" (12 [14, 16] cm), shape the armhole by binding off every 2 rows at each side: 2 sts 2 times and 1 st 2 times. 45 (51, 57) sts.
At 7¾" (9, 10¼)" (20 [23, 26] cm), bind off the center 13 (15, 17) sts. Work 2 rows then bind off 5 sts once for the neckline.
At 8¼" (9½, 10½)" (21 [24, 27] cm), bind off all 11 (13, 15) shoulder sts.

Right Front

Cast on 44 (50, 56) sts on larger needles. Work ⅜" (1 cm) in garter st then change to St st.

At 4¾" (5½, 6¼)" (12 [14, 16] cm), shape the diagonal neckline by dec 1 st in from the right edge every other row as follows: 2 st, 13 (15, 17) times then 1 st once. (*See Special Stitches*) and, **AT THE SAME TIME**, bind off along the armhole as for the back.

At 8¼" (9½, 10½)" (21 [24, 27] cm), bind off all 11 (13, 15) shoulder sts.

Left Front

Work the same as right front, reversing shaping.

Sleeves

Cast on 38 (42, 46) sts on smaller needles. Work ⅜" (1 cm) in garter st, then change to larger needles and work in St st. Inc 1 st at each side as follows:

Newborn: Every 7 rows 5 times. 48 sts.

3 months: Every 8 rows 6 times. 54 sts.

6 months: Every 8 rows 7 times. 60 sts.

At 4¼" (6, 6¾)" (11 [15, 17] cm), bind off at each side every other rows as follows: 2 sts 2 times then 1 st 2 times. Bind off the rest.

Finishing

Sew the shoulders.

Border: Pick up and k 28 (34, 40) sts on smaller needles along the straight edge of the right front then 35 (38, 41) sts along the diagonal neckline, 28 (30, 32) sts on the back neckline, 35 (38, 41) st along the left front, and 28 (34, 40) sts along the straight edge. Work ⅜" (1 cm) in garter st and bind off.

Seam sleeves to armhole then seam sleeve and side seams. Sew on 3 snaps to keep the fronts closed.

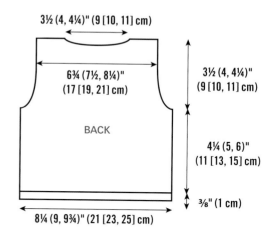

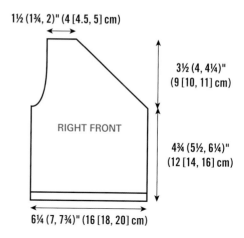

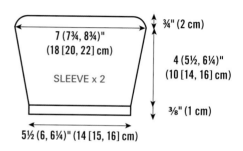

28 – Sleepy Feline Friend

Yarn: Sport weight (#2 Fine)
Size: About 15¾" (40 cm) tall
Needles: Size US 2 (3 mm)

29 – Contrast Banded Cardigan

Yarn: Sport weight (#2 Fine)
Sizes: Newborn (3 months, 6 months)
Needles: Size US 1 (2.5mm) and Size US 2 (3 mm)

30 – Contrast Banded Bloomers

Yarn: Sport weight (#2 Fine)
Sizes: Newborn (3 months, 6 months)
Needles: Size US 1 (2.5mm) and Size US 2 (3 mm)

31 – Simple Knitted Baby Socks

Yarn: Sport weight (#2 Fine)
Sizes: Newborn (3 months, 6 months)
Needles: Size US 1 (2.5mm) and Size US 2 (3 mm)

28 - *Sleepy Feline Friend*

This very tired plush cat is fun to knit with contrasting colors. The front is knit in gray while the back is knit in white. A pop of color has been added to the ears.

SIZE
- About 15¾" (40 cm) tall

YARN
- Sport weight (#2 Fine)
  Phildar Lambswool (51% wool, 49% acrylic; 147 yds [134 m]/1.76 oz [50 g]): Flanelle (MC), Dragée (CC1), and Blanc (CC2), 1 skein each

NEEDLES
- Size US 2 (3 mm)
  Adjust needle size if necessary to obtain the correct gauge.

NOTIONS
- 20" (50 cm) of pink satin ribbon; fiber stuffing; tapestry needle

GAUGE
- 26 sts and 36 rows = 4" (10 cm) in St st

NOTES
- Cat is worked following the 3 charts for the body, arms, and ears

---

Cat

As an example of how to work using charts, for the front, cast on 7 sts in MC. Work in St st. Inc 1 st at each side on rows 3, 5, and 7. 13 sts. Continue working straight. Inc 1 st at the start of row 64. Put on hold at the end of row 66. Work the other leg reversing the shaping. Cast on 1 st and then work on the sts on hold. 29 sts. Continue straight. To shape the shoulders cast off 5 sts on each side of row 102 then bind off 2 st at each side of row 104.

Shape the cheeks by increasing 1 st each side of row 106, 107, 108, 109, 110, 112, and 116. 29 sts.

Shape the top of the head by dec 1 st at each side of rows 128, 130, 132, then dec 2 sts at each side of rows 136 and 138. Bind off the remaining 11 sts on row 140.

Work a second side but in CC2.

Work 2 arms in blanc and 2 arms in MC.

Work 4 ears in CC1.

Finishing

Sew the ears RS together leaving the bottom open. Turn RS out. Sew an arm on each side of the body. Pin an ear on each side of the head on one of the body pieces. Place the body pieces RS together and sew around leaving an opening under one arm. Turn inside out and stuff. Sew closed.

Embroider the MC face and the claws on the feet using straight stitches in CC2 (see photo). Sew the inside of the ears with MC as shown. Tie the ribbon around the neck.

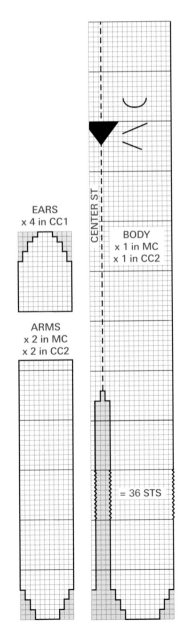

EARS
x 4 in CC1

ARMS
x 2 in MC
x 2 in CC2

CENTER ST

BODY
x 1 in MC
x 1 in CC2

= 36 STS

29 - Contrast Banded Cardigan

Add visual interest to the waistband, cuffs, and trim of this classic style cardigan with a contrast color. Any color combination will do!

SIZES
- Newborn (3 months, 6 months)

YARN
- Sport weight (#2 Fine)
  Phildar Lambswool (51% wool, 49% acrylic; 147 yds [134 m]/1.76 oz [50 g])
  Pink cardigan: Dragée (MC), 2 skeins; Flanelle (CC), 1 skein
  Grey cardigan: Flanelle (MC) 2 skeins; Blanc (CC), 1 skein

NEEDLES
- Size US 1 (2.5 mm) and Size US 2 (3 mm)
  Adjust needle size if necessary to obtain the correct gauge.

NOTIONS
- Five buttons; tapestry needle

GAUGE
- 26 sts and 36 rows = 4" (10 cm) in St st on larger needles

SPECIAL STITCHES
- **To dec 1 st at each side of a row:** k1, k2tog, work to last 3 sts, SKP, k1
- **To dec 2 sts at each side of row:** k1, k3tog, work to last 4 sts, double dec, k1
- **SKP:** sl 1, k1, pass slipped st over
- **Double dec:** sl 1, k2tog pass slipped st over

Back
Cast on 63 (69, 75) sts in CC on larger needles. Work ⅝" (1.5 cm) of 1 x 1 ribbing then k 1 row on the WS working 1 dec in the middle of the row. Change to St st and MC. 62 (68, 74) sts.
At 5 (6, 6¾)" (13 [15, 17] cm), shape the armholes: dec every 2 rows at each side as follows: 2 sts 2 times then 1 st 3 times. 48 (54, 60) sts.
At 8¾ (9¾, 11)" (22 [25, 28] cm), bind off the center 14 (16, 18) sts and work each side separately. Work 2 rows then shape the neckline by binding off 5 sts at the neckline.
At 9 (10¼, 11½)" (23 [26, 29] cm) long, bind off the remaining 12 (14, 16) shoulder sts.

Right Front
Cast on 31 (34, 37) sts in CC on larger needles. Work ⅝" (1.5 cm) of 1 x 1 ribbing then 1 k row on the WS. Change to St st and MC.
At 5 (6, 6¾)" (13 [15, 17] cm), shape the neckline: dec 1 st at the right edge every 2 rows 12 (13, 14) times and dec at the left side to shape the armholes as for the back.
At 9 (10¼, 11½)" (23 [26, 29] cm), bind off 12 (14, 16) shoulder sts.

Left Front
Work the same, reversing the shaping.

Sleeves
Cast on 38 (42, 46) sts in CC on smaller needles. Work ⅝" (1.5 cm) of 1 x 1 ribbing then k 1 row on the WS. Change to St st and MC with larger needles. as follows:
Newborn: Inc 1 st at each side every 4 rows 8 times. 54 sts.
3 months: Inc 1 st at each side every 5 rows 9 times. 60 sts.
6 months: Inc 1 st at each side every 5 rows 10 times). 66 sts.
At 4¼ (6, 6¾)" (11 [15, 17] cm), bind off at each side as follows: 2 sts 2 times and 1 st 3 times, then bind off the remaining sts.

Pockets
Cast on 19 sts in MC on larger needles. Work 2" (5 cm) in St st then change to smaller needles 2.5 and CC and p one row on the RS. Work ⅝" (1.5 cm) of 1 x 1 ribbing and bind off.

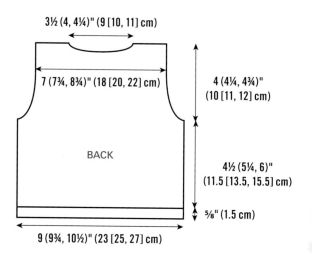

3½ (4, 4¼)" (9 [10, 11] cm)

7 (7¾, 8¾)" (18 [20, 22] cm)

4 (4¼, 4¾)"
(10 [11, 12] cm)

BACK

4½ (5¼, 6)"
(11.5 [13.5, 15.5] cm)

⅝" (1.5 cm)

9 (9¾, 10½)" (23 [25, 27] cm)

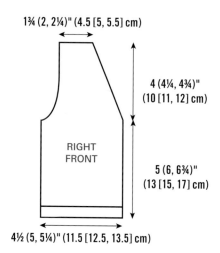

1¾ (2, 2¼)" (4.5 [5, 5.5] cm)

4 (4¼, 4¾)"
(10 [11, 12] cm)

RIGHT
FRONT

5 (6, 6¾)"
(13 [15, 17] cm)

4½ (5, 5¼)" (11.5 [12.5, 13.5] cm)

Finishing

Sew the shoulders.

Border: Pick up and k 40 (46, 52) sts in CC, on smaller needles, along the straight edge on the right front, 27 (30, 33) sts along the neckline diagonal, 27 (29, 31) sts along the back neckline, 27 (30, 33) sts along the left front diagonal then 40 (46, 52) sts along the left front straight edge. K 1 row on the WS then work ⅝" (1.5 cm) of 1 x 1 ribbing and bind off. **AT THE SAME TIME**, starting on row 2, work 5, 1 st buttonholes with the first, 4 sts in from the end and the remaining spaced: 8 (9, alternate 10 and 11 sts).

Seam sleeves to armhole then seam the sleeve and sides. Sew the pockets to the fronts and sew on the buttons.

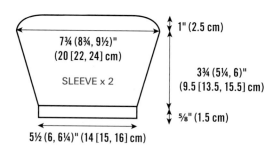

1" (2.5 cm)

7¾ (8¾, 9½)"
(20 [22, 24] cm)

3¾ (5¼, 6)"
(9.5 [13.5, 15.5] cm)

SLEEVE x 2

⅝" (1.5 cm)

5½ (6, 6¼)" (14 [15, 16] cm)

30 - *Contrast Banded Bloomers*

SIZES
• Newborn (3 months, 6 months)

YARN
• Sport weight (#2 Fine)
Phildar Lambswool (51% wool, 49% acrylic; 147 yds [134 m]/1.76 oz [50 g])
Pink bloomers: Dragée (MC) and Flanelle (CC), 1 skein each
Grey bloomers: Flanelle (MC) and Blanc (CC), 1 skein each

NEEDLES
• Size US 1 (2.5 mm) and Size US 2 (3 mm)
Adjust needle size if necessary to obtain the correct gauge.

NOTIONS
• Elastic thread for waist; two buttons; tapestry needle

GAUGE
• 26 sts and 36 rows = 4" (10 cm) in St st on larger needles

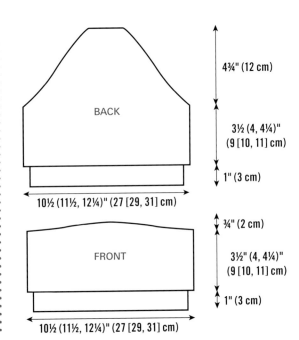

Front
Cast on 72 (78, 84) sts in MC on smaller needles. Work 1" (3 cm) of 1 x 1 ribbing. Change to larger needles and work in St st.
At 4¾ (5, 5½)" (12 [13, 14] cm), bind off every 2 rows as follows:
Newborn: 11 sts then 10 sts then 8 sts.
3 months: 12 sts, then 11 sts then 9 sts.
6 months: 13 sts, then 10 sts then 10 sts.
Bind off the remaining 14 sts.

Back
Cast on 72 (78, 84) sts in MC on smaller needles. Work 1" (3 cm) 1 x 1 ribbing. Change to larger needles and work in St st.
At 4¾ (5, 5½)" (12 [13, 14] cm), for all sizes: bind off 1 st at each side, then work 6 rows, bind off 1 st 1 time, work 4 rows, bind off 1 st 1 time. Then every 2 rows bind off (each size differently) as follows:
Newborn: 1 st 3 times and then 2 sts 9 times, then *1 st 1 time 2 sts 1 time* 2 times.
3 months: 21 st 2 times and 2 sts 14 times
6 months: 1 st 1 time and 2 sts 11 times, *2 sts 1 time, 3 sts 1 time *2 times.
Bind off the remaining 12 sts.

Finishing
Border Front: Pick up and k 72 (78, 84) sts in CC along the shaped top row. K 1 row on the WS then 4 rows of 1 x 1 ribbing and bind off.
Border Back: Work as for the front border, pick up and k 96 (102, 108) sts and working 2, 1 st buttonholes on row 2 on either side of the 12 center sts.
Sew the sides. Bring the back to the front and sew the 2 buttons opposite the buttonholes.

31 - *Simple Knitted Baby Socks*

It's always handy to have an extra pair of socks to slip on your little one's feet. Knit several pairs of these classic socks in a variety of color to match every outfit.

SIZES

- Newborn (3 months, 6 months)

YARN

- Sport weight (#2 Fine)
  Phildar Lambswool (51% wool, 49% acrylic; 147 yds [134 m]/1.76 oz [50 g])
  Pink socks: Dragée (MC) and Flanelle (CC), 1 skein each
  Grey socks: Flanelle (MC) and Blanc (CC), 1 skein each

NEEDLES

- Size US 1 (2.5 mm) and Size US 2 (3 mm)
  Adjust needle size if necessary to obtain the correct gauge.

NOTIONS

- Tapestry needle

GAUGE

- 26 sts and 36 rows = 4" (10 cm) in St st on larger needles

Socks

Cast on 32 (40, 48) sts in CC using smaller needles. Work ⅝" (1.5 cm) of 1 x 1 ribbing, then k 1 row on the WS. Change to larger needles and work in St st with MC.

At 2½ (3, 3¼)" (6.5 [7.5, 8.5] cm), work the half heel in St st with CC just on the first 8 sts. Work short rows working 1 less st every other row 5 times, then working 1 more st every 2 rows 5 times. Put those sts on hold and repeat on the last 8 sts for the other heel half.

For the foot, work in St st with on all the sts in MC for 1¼ (1¾, 2¼)" (3.5 [4.5, 5.5] cm).

For the foot, work in St st with CC shaping as follows: k 6 (8, 10), k2tog, 1 skp, k 12 (16, 20) sts, k2tog, 1 skp, k 6 (8, 10) sts. Placing the dec on top of each other, repeat the dec every 2 rows, 5 (7, 9) more times.

Finishing

Cut the yarn and thread through all the sts pulling tightly. Seam the sock closed.

Little Flower

32 – Embellished Tunic Dress

Yarn: Sport weight (#2 Fine)
Sizes: 3 months (6 months, 12 months)
Needles: Size US 2 (3 mm)

33 – Embellished Leggings

Yarn: Sport weight (#2 Fine)
Sizes: 3 months (6 months, 12 months)
Needles: Size US 1 (2.5 mm) and Size US 2 (3 mm)

32 - *Embellished Tunic Dress*

Add sweet little spring-inspired flowers to a tunic dress. The dress itself is knit while the flowers are made using basic crochet stitches.

SIZES
- 3 months (6 months, 12 months)

YARN
- Sport weight (#2 Fine)
  Phildar Lambswool (51% wool, 49% acrylic; 147 yds [134 m]/1.76 oz [50 g]): Ecru (MC), 2 (2, 3) skeins; Pensée (CC1), Freesia (CC2), and Fuchsia (CC3), 1 skein each

NEEDLES
- Size US 2 (3 mm)
  Adjust needle size if necessary to obtain the correct gauge.

NOTIONS
- Size US B-1 (2.5 mm) crochet hook; size garment snaps; tapestry needle

GAUGE
- 26 sts and 36 rows = 4" (10 cm) in St st

SPECIAL STITCHES
- **Single crochet:** sc
- **Double crochet:** dc
- **Chain stitch (crochet):** ch st
- **Crochet Picot:** *1 sc in each of the next 3 sts, ch 3. Repeat from *working the first sc in the same st as the last sc worked.

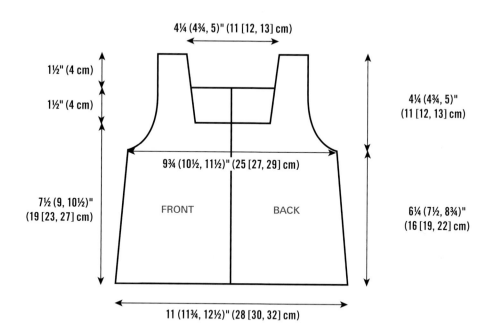

4¼ (4¾, 5)" (11 [12, 13] cm)

1½" (4 cm)

1½" (4 cm)

4¼ (4¾, 5)"
(11 [12, 13] cm)

9¾ (10½, 11½)" (25 [27, 29] cm)

7½ (9, 10½)"
(19 [23, 27] cm)

FRONT

BACK

6¼ (7½, 8¾)"
(16 [19, 22] cm)

11 (11¾, 12½)" (28 [30, 32] cm)

Front

Cast on 74 (80, 86) sts in MC. Work in St st and dec 1 st at each side every 14 (16, 18) rows 4 times. 66 (72, 78) sts.

At 6¼ (7½, 8¾)" (16 [19, 22] cm), to shape the armholes: bind off every 2 rows at each side as follows: 3 sts 1 time, 2 sts 2 times, and 1 st 3 times. 46 (52, 58) sts.

At 7½ (9, 10½)" (19 [23, 27] cm), bind off the center 24 (26, 28) sts. Shape the neckline by binding off 1 st every 6 rows 3 times.

At 10½ (12¼, 13¾)" (27 [31, 35] cm), bind off 8 (10, 12) shoulder sts.

Half Back

Cast on 38 (41, 44) sts and work in St st working the same dec on the left side and the armhole as for back. 24 (27, 30) sts.

At 9 (10½, 12¼)" (23 [27, 31] cm), shape the neckline by binding off at the RS: 15 (16, 17) sts, work 4 rows and bind off 1 st.

At 10½ (12¼, 13¾)" (27 [31, 35] cm), bind off 8 (10, 12) shoulder sts.

Work the other half of the back reversing the shaping.

Flowers

Crochet 1 flower in each CC1, CC2, and CC3 using a Size US B-1 (2.25 mm) crochet hook as follows: make a loop, *ch3, dc, ch3, sc in the loop* 5 times.

Finishing

Sew the shoulders and the sides. Work a border around the openings with a row of sc in MC then a row of picots. Sew on snaps on the back. Sew the 3 flowers in front.

33 - *Embellished Leggings*

Designed to be worn with the matching tunic dress, these footed
leggings are embellished with crochet flowers on each foot.

SIZES
- 3 months (6 months, 12 months)

YARN
- Sport weight (#2 Fine)
  Phildar Lambswool (51% wool, 49% acrylic; 147 yds
  [134 m]/1.76 oz [50 g]): Ecru (MC), 3 (3, 4) skeins;
  Pensée (CC1), and Fuchsia (CC2), 1 skein each

NEEDLES
- Size US 1 (2.5 mm) and Size US 2 (3 mm)
  *Adjust needle size if necessary to obtain the
  correct gauge.*

NOTIONS
- Size US B-1 (2.25 mm) crochet hook; elastic thread;
  tapestry needle

GAUGE
- 26 sts and 36 rows = 4" (10 cm) in St st on
  larger needles

NOTES
- Leggings are worked in one piece, starting at the
  lower left leg

SPECIAL STITCHES
- **Single crochet:** sc
- **Double crochet:** dc
- **Chain stitch (crochet):** ch st

Back
Cast on 25 (28, 31) sts in MC on larger needles. Work in St st.
Inc 1 st each side every 6 (7, 9) rows 8 times. 16 (17¼, 18½)" (41
[44, 47] sts). At 5½ (6¾, 7¾)" (14 [17, 20] cm), put the sts
on hold.
Work the right leg the same then take up the left leg sts. 82 (88,
94) st. Shape the crotch by dec 1 st on either side of the center
2 sts each row 3 times, then 1 st every 2 rows 3 times. 70 (76,
82) sts.
At 11½ (13, 14½)" (29 [33, 37] cm), change to smaller needles.
Work 1" (3 cm) of 1 x 1 ribbing and bind off.

Front
Work as for the back.

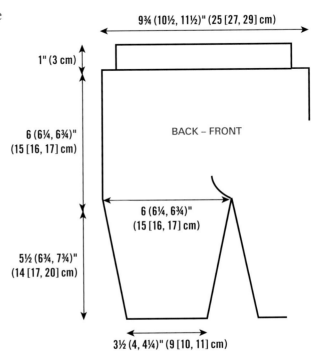

9¾ (10½, 11½)" (25 [27, 29] cm)

1" (3 cm)

BACK – FRONT

6 (6¼, 6¾)"
(15 [16, 17] cm)

6 (6¼, 6¾)"
(15 [16, 17] cm)

5½ (6¾, 7¾)"
(14 [17, 20] cm)

3½ (4, 4¼)" (9 [10, 11] cm)

Foot

Sole of Foot: Cast on 12 (14, 14) sts in MC on larger needles. Work 3¼ (3¾, 4)" (8.5 [9.5, 10.5] cm) in St st and bind off.

Side of Foot: Cast on 56 (66, 72) sts with MC on larger needles. Work 1 (1¼, 1½)" (3 [3.5, 4] cm) of St st and bind off.

Top of Foot: Cast on 12 (14, 14) sts in MC on larger needles. Work in St st. Starting on row 11 (14, 17), dec 1 st at each side every 2 rows, 3 times then 1 st 1 time on the next row. Bind off the remaining sts.

Flowers

Crochet 1 flower with CC1 and 1 flower in CC2: Make a loop and with Size US B-1 (2.5 mm) crochet hook, *ch 3, 1 dc, ch 3, 1 sc in the loop* 5 times.

Finishing

Sew the sides and inner leg.

Sew the side of the foot into a tube then sew around the sole.

Attach the top to the side. Place a foot at the bottom of each leg, gathering it a bit if needed.

Sew 1 flower on each foot. Thread several rows of elastic thread under the ribbing on the waist.

Cute in Cables

34 – Braided Sprite Hat

Yarn: Worsted weight (#4 Medium)

Size: Newborn to 3 months

Needles: Size US 2 (3 mm) and Size US 4 (3.5 mm)

35 – Braided Thumbless Mittens

Yarn: Worsted weight (#4 Medium)

Size: Newborn to 3 months

Needles: Size US 2 (3 mm) and Size US 4 (3.5 mm)

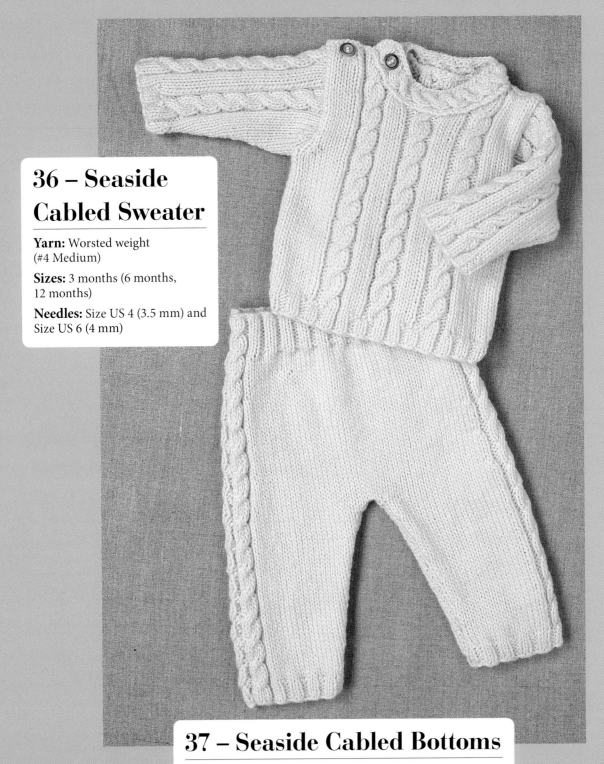

36 – Seaside Cabled Sweater

Yarn: Worsted weight (#4 Medium)

Sizes: 3 months (6 months, 12 months)

Needles: Size US 4 (3.5 mm) and Size US 6 (4 mm)

37 – Seaside Cabled Bottoms

Yarn: Worsted weight (#4 Medium)

Sizes: 3 months (6 months, 12 months)

Needles: Size US 4 (3.5 mm) and Size US 6 (4 mm)

39 – Zip-Up Cabled Hooded Baby Bag

Yarn: Bulky weight (#5 Bulky)
Size: Newborn to 3 months
Needles: Size US 2 (3 mm) and Size US 6 (4 mm)

38 – Arctic Bear with Scarf

Yarn: Worsted weight (#4 Medium)
Size: About 7" (18 cm) tall
Needles: Size US 2 (3 mm) and Size US 6 (4 mm)

34 - *Braided Sprite Hat*

This simply cabled hat is a great beginner project. The baby who wears this will look adorable with the cute pointed top. Make the matching thumbless mittens for a great winter set.

SIZE
- Newborn to 3 months

YARN
- Worsted weight (#4 Medium)
  Phildar Quiétude (50% wool, 50% acrylic; 98 yds [90 m]/1.76 oz [50 g]): Céladon, 2 skeins

NEEDLES
- Size US 2 (3 mm) and Size US 4 (3.5 mm)

NOTIONS
- Cable needle; tapestry needle

SPECIAL STITCHES
- **Cables:** Work the first 10 sts of the chart repeating it every 12 rows (see chart on page 87)

Bonnet
Cast on 82 sts on smaller needles. Work 2¾" (7 cm) of 2 x 2 ribbing.
Change to larger needles and work 32 sts in St st, p2, k2, cable 10 sts, 4 sts in ribbing, 32 sts in St st.
At 4¾" (12 cm), start the crown shaping: 1 edge stitch, *k2tog, k 6 sts* 10 times, 1 edge st. Place the dec over the previous dec every 2 rows 5 times. Thread the yarn through the remaining 12 sts tightly and fix the tail. Seam the bonnet reversing the seam side on half the ribbing on the sides.

35 - *Braided Thumbless Mittens*

SIZE
- Newborn to 3 months

YARN
- Worsted weight (#4 Medium)
  Phildar Quiétude (50% wool, 50% acrylic; 98 yds [90 m]/1.76 oz [50 g]): Céladon, 1 skein

NEEDLES
- Size US 2 (3 mm) and Size US 4 (3.5 mm)

NOTIONS
- Cable needle; tapestry needle

SPECIAL STITCHES
- **Cables:** Work the first 10 sts of the chart repeating it every 12 rows (see chart on page 87)

Mittens
Cast on 16 sts on smaller needles. Work 2¼" (6 cm) of 2 x 2 ribbing.
Change to larger needles and work 3 sts in St st, 10 sts in cable, 3 sts St st.
At 4¾" (12 cm), dec1 st on each side every 2 rows 3 times. Bind off the remaining sts.
Work the 2nd half the same. Place the 2 pieces RS together and seam around, reversing the seam side on the lower half of the ribbing.
Join the 2 mittens with a long-twisted cord.

36 - *Seaside Cabled Sweater*

With the look of a classic fisherman's sweater and matching bottoms, this hearty pullover is sure to become a treasured family heirloom.

SIZES

- 3 months (6 months, 12 months)

YARN

- Worsted weight (#4 Medium)
  Phildar Quiétude (50% wool, 50% acrylic; 98 yds
  [90 m]/1.76 oz [50 g]): Ecru, 3 (3, 4) skeins

NEEDLES

- Size US 4 (3.5 mm) and Size US 6 (4 mm)
  Adjust needle size if necessary to obtain the correct gauge.

NOTIONS

- Cable needle; two buttons; tapestry needle

GAUGE

- 32 st cable panel = 4¼" (11 cm) on larger needles
- 22 sts and 28 rows = 4" (10 cm) in St st on larger needles

SPECIAL STITCHES

- **Cable panel:** Work 32 sts according to the chart repeating the rows between *

Back

Cast on 58 (62, 66) sts on smaller needles. Work ¾" (2 cm) of 2 x 2 ribbing. Change to larger needles and work as follows: 13 (15, 17) sts in St st, 32 sts cable chart, 13 (15, 17) St sts.
At 5 (6, 6¾)" (13 [15, 17] cm), shape the armholes. Bind off at each side every 2 rows: 2 sts 1 time, 1 st 2 times. 50 (54, 58) sts. When it is 9½ (10½, 11¾)" (24 [27, 30] cm), bind off the center 12 (14, 16) sts and then work each side separately. Work 2 rows, then bind off 6 sts at the neckline.
At 9¾ (11, 12¼)" (25 [28, 31] cm), bind off all 13 (14, 15) sts.

Front

Work as for the back.
At 8¼ (9½, 10½)" (21 [24, 27] cm), bind off the center 12 (14, 16) sts and work each side separately. Bind off at the neckline every 2 rows as follows: 3 st, 2 sts, then 1 st.
At 9½ (10½, 11¾)" (24 [27, 30] cm), make a 1 st buttonhole in the middle of the left shoulder.
At 9¾ (11, 12¼)" (25 [28, 31] cm), bind off the remaining 13 (14, 15) shoulder sts.

Sleeves

Cast on 42 (44, 46) sts on smaller needles. Work ¾" (2 cm) of 2 x 2 ribbing. Change to larger needles, and work 5 (6, 7) sts in St st, 32 sts in cable chart, 5 (6, 7) St sts.
Inc 1 st at each side every 4 rows, 8 (9, 10) times. 58 (62, 66) sts.
At 6 (6¾, 7)" (15 [17, 18] cm), bind off 2 sts one time, then 1 st 2 times at each side every 2 rows. Bind off the rest.

CABLE PANEL CHART

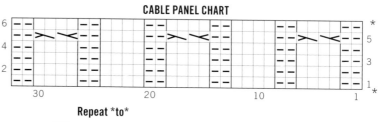

Repeat *to*

☐ K on RS, p on WS

▭ P on RS, k on WS

⟩⟨ Sl 2 sts on cable needle and hold in front, k2, then k2 from cable needle

36 - Seaside Cabled Sweater (continued)

Finishing

Button Band: Pick up and k 13 (14, 15) sts on smaller needles along the left back shoulder. Work ¾" (2 cm) of 2 x 2 ribbing and bind off.

Neckline Border: Cast on 8 sts on smaller needles. Work the first 8 sts of the cable chart. At ⅜" (1 cm), work a 1 st buttonhole in the center of the border. Bind off when the border is the same length as the neckline (including the button band).

Sew the right shoulders, the neckline border and the buttons. Sew sleeves to the armhole. Seam the sleeves and sides. Sew on the buttons.

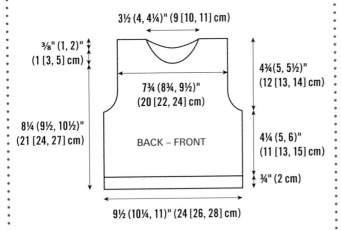

3½ (4, 4¼)" (9 [10, 11] cm)

⅜" (1, 2)" (1 [3, 5] cm)

4¾ (5, 5½)" (12 [13, 14] cm)

7¾ (8¾, 9½)" (20 [22, 24] cm)

8¼ (9½, 10½)" (21 [24, 27] cm)

BACK – FRONT

4¼ (5, 6)" (11 [13, 15] cm)

¾" (2 cm)

9½ (10¼, 11)" (24 [26, 28] cm)

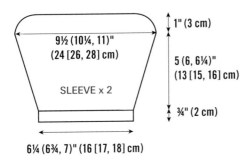

9½ (10¼, 11)" (24 [26, 28] cm)

1" (3 cm)

5 (6, 6¼)" (13 [15, 16] cm)

SLEEVE x 2

¾" (2 cm)

6¼ (6¾, 7)" (16 [17, 18] cm)

37 - Seaside Cabled Bottoms

SIZES
- 3 months (6 months, 12 months)

YARN
- Worsted weight (#4 Medium) Phildar Quiétude (50% wool, 50% acrylic; 98 yds [90 m]/1.76 oz [50 g]): Ecru, 3 (3, 4) skeins

NEEDLES
- Size US 4 (3.5 mm) and Size US 6 (4 mm) *Adjust needle size if necessary to obtain the correct gauge.*

NOTIONS
- Cable needle; elastic thread; tapestry needle

GAUGE
- 22 sts and 28 rows = 4" (10 cm) in St st on larger needles

NOTES
- Pants are started at the lower left leg and worked upward

SPECIAL STITCHES
- **Cable panel:** Work 8 sts according to the chart repeating the rows between *

Back

Cast on 22 (24, 26) sts on smaller needles. Work 14 (16, 18) sts in 2 x 2 ribbing starting with p2 (k2, p2), 8 cable sts. At ¾" (2 cm), change to larger needles and work in St st above the ribbing. Inc 1 st along the RS every 3 (4, 6) rows 7 times. Put the 29 (31, 33) sts on hold at 4¼ (5½, 6¾)" (11 [14, 17] cm).

Work the right leg reversing shaping then take up the left leg sts. 58 (62, 66) sts. Dec 1 st 8 sts in from each side every 7 rows 5 times. 48 (52, 56) sts.

At 9½ (11, 12½0" (24 [28, 32] cm), change to smaller needles, work 1" (3 cm) of 2 x 2 ribbing and bind off.

Front

Work as for the back.

Finishing

Sew the seams. Thread several rows of elastic thread under the waistband.

38 - Arctic Bear with Scarf

SIZE
- About 7" (18 cm) tall

YARN
- Worsted weight (#4 Medium) Phildar Quiétude (50% wool, 50% acrylic; 98 yds [90 m]/1.76 oz [50 g]): Céladon and Ecru, 1 skein each

NEEDLES
- Size US 2 (3 mm) and Size US 6 (4 mm) *Adjust needle size if necessary to obtain the correct gauge.*

NOTIONS
- Fiber stuffing; tapestry needle

GAUGE
- 20 sts and 26 rows = 4" (10 cm) in St st on larger needles

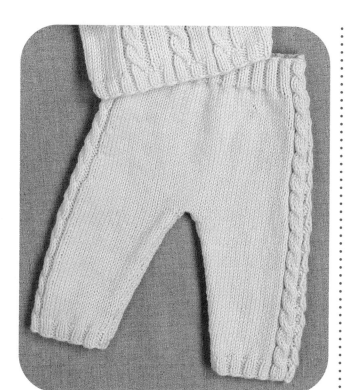

PANTS CABLE PANEL CHART

Repeat from * to *

K on RS, p on WS

P on RS, k on WS

Sl 2 sts on cable needle and hold in front, k2, then k2 from cable needle

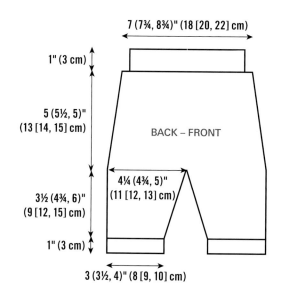

7 (7¾, 8¾)" (18 [20, 22] cm)

1" (3 cm)

5 (5½, 5)" (13 [14, 15] cm)

BACK – FRONT

3½ (4¾, 6)" (9 [12, 15] cm)

4¼ (4¾, 5)" (11 [12, 13] cm)

1" (3 cm)

3 (3½, 4)" (8 [9, 10] cm)

Ears
Cast on 6 sts on larger needle and work in garter st. On row 6 bind the first 5 sts over the 6th and attach the end firmly.

Body
Start on the left leg. Cast on 8 sts. Work in St st for 6 rows. Put the sts on hold. Work the right leg the same, cast on 1 st for the crotch and take up the left leg. On row 20, cast on 6 st at each side for the arms and work 10 rows. Bind off 8 st at each side then shape the head as follows: inc 1 st at each side on row 31 and 33. Dec 1 st at each side on row 41, 43, 44, and 45. Bind off the remaining sts.

Work a second part the same. Pin the ears to the head. Place the other half RS together. Sew around the head catching the ears and then the shoulders.

Hands
Pick up and k 16 st at the end of each arm. Work 12 rows in garter st, sl the yarn through the sts and pull tight. Seam the hands, arms and sides leaving an opening.

Feet
Pick up and k 14 sts at the end of each leg. Work 12 rows in garter st. Sl the yarn through the sts and attach firmly. Seam the legs and feet. Stuff. Sew the opening. Embroider the head.

Scarf
Cast on 4 sts using smaller needles. Work 9¾" (25 cm) in garter st and bind off.

39 - Zip-Up Cabled Hooded Baby Bag

Combine traditionally braided cables with the ease of a zip-up baby bag for a project that keeps your newborn cozy and comfortable.

SIZE
- Newborn to 3 months

YARN
- Bulky weight (#5 Bulky)
  Phildar Partner 6 (50% polyamide, 25% wool, 25% acrylic; 71 yds [65 m]/1.76 oz [50 g]): Ecru, 9 skeins

NEEDLES
- Size US 2 (3 mm) and Size US 6 (4 mm)
  Adjust needle size if necessary to obtain the correct gauge.

NOTIONS
- Cable needle; One 17¾" (45 cm) zipper; tapestry needle

GAUGE
- 18 sts and 27 rows = 4" (10 cm) in St st on larger needles

SPECIAL STITCHES
- **Cable panel:** Work 10 st and 12 row repeat of chart

Back
Cast on 60 sts on larger needles. Work 9 sts in St st, p2, k2, 10 sts in cable pattern, 14 sts in 2 x 2 ribbing, 10 st in cable pattern, 4 sts in 2 x 2 ribbing, 9 sts St st. Inc 1 st every 8 rows at each side 4 times. 68 sts.
At 5½" (14 cm), dec 1 st at each side every 6 rows 7 times. 54 sts.
At 15" (38 cm), shape the armholes. Bind off at each side every 2 rows: 3 sts 1 time, 2 sts 1 time, 1 st 1 time. 42 sts.
At 18¾" (48 cm), bind off the center 16 sts and work each side separately.
At 19¼" (49 cm), bind off the remaining 13 sts on the shoulder.

Right Front
Cast on 32 sts on smaller needles. Work as follows: 1 edge st, 8 sts of 2 x 2 ribbing starting with p2, 10 st of cable pattern, 4 sts 2 x 2 ribbing, 9 sts in St st.
Work the shaping as on the left side of the back. 23 sts after the armhole shaping.
At 17¼" (44 cm), shape the neckline and bind off every 2 rows: 3 sts 1 time, 2 sts 2 times, and 1 st 1 time.
At 19¼" (49 cm), bind off all 13 shoulder sts

Left Front
Work the same as the right front, reversing the shaping.

Sleeves

Cast on 32 sts on smaller needles. Work 2¼" (6 cm) of 2 x 2 ribbing. Change to larger needles and continue in St st, increasing 1 st at each side every 5 rows. 42 sts.
At 6¾" (17 cm), bind off at each side every 2 rows: 3 sts 1 time, 2 sts 1 time, and 1 st 1 time. Bind of the remaining sts.

Hood

Cast on 94 sts on smaller needles. Work ¾" (2 cm) of 2 x 2 ribbing. Change to larger needles and work as follows: 38 sts in St st, p2, k2, 10 cable pattern sts, 4 sts 2 x 2 ribbing, 38 sts in St st.
At 4¾" (12 cm), bind off 9 sts at each side every 2 rows 4 times. Bind off the remaining 22 sts.

Finishing

Front Border: With smaller needles pick up and k 82 sts along the edge of each front. K 1 row on the WS then bind off purlwise on the RS. Sew the shoulders. Seam the back of the hood and seam to the neckline. Seam the sleeves to the armhole. Seam the sides and the arms. Seam in the zipper between the 2 fronts.

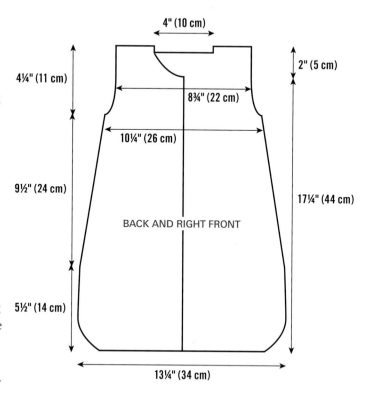

4" (10 cm)

2" (5 cm)

4¼" (11 cm)

8¾" (22 cm)

10¼" (26 cm)

9½" (24 cm)

17¼" (44 cm)

BACK AND RIGHT FRONT

5½" (14 cm)

13¼" (34 cm)

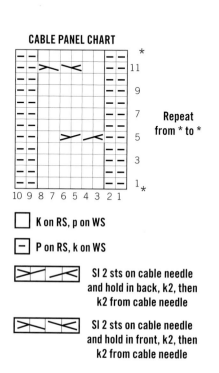

CABLE PANEL CHART

11
9
7
5
3
1

Repeat
from * to *

10 9 8 7 6 5 4 3 2 1

□ K on RS, p on WS

— P on RS, k on WS

Sl 2 sts on cable needle
and hold in back, k2, then
k2 from cable needle

Sl 2 sts on cable needle
and hold in front, k2, then
k2 from cable needle

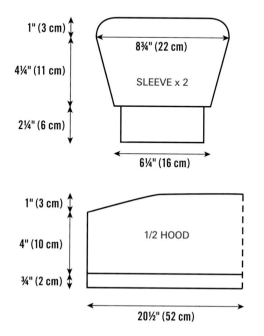

1" (3 cm)

8¾" (22 cm)

4¼" (11 cm)

SLEEVE x 2

2¼" (6 cm)

6¼" (16 cm)

1" (3 cm)

4" (10 cm)

1/2 HOOD

¾" (2 cm)

20½" (52 cm)

40 - X & O Hooded Jacket

Yarn: Bulky weight (#5 Bulky)

Sizes: 3 months (6 months, 12 months, 24 months)

Needles: Size US 7 (4.5 mm) and Size US 8 (5 mm)

Snuggly and warm

41, 42 & 43 – My First Scarf, Simple Cap with Earflaps, and Tasseled Mittens

Yarn: Bulky weight (#5 Bulky)

Size: One size

Needles: Size US 8 (5 mm)

40 - *X & O Hooded Jacket*

Show off your child's playful spirit with this fun design. The cabled pattern is mirrored on either side of the button band and the hood is embellished with blanket stitch for a unique contrast.

SIZES
- 3 months (6 months, 12 months, 24 months)

YARN
- Bulky weight (#5 Bulky)
  Phildar Partner 6 (50% polyamide, 25% wool, 25% acrylic; 71 yds [65 m]/1.76 oz [50 g]): Naturel (MC), 6 (7, 8, 9) skeins; Ecru (CC), 1 skein

NEEDLES
- Size US 7 (4.5 mm) and Size US 8 (5 mm)
  Adjust needle size if necessary to obtain the correct gauge.

NOTIONS
- Cable needle; five buttons; tapestry needle

GAUGE
- 20 sts and 24 rows = 4" (10 cm) in St st on larger needles

SPECIAL STITCHES
- **Cable panel:** Work 19 st of Chart A or B repeating the 12 rows between * and *

NOTES
- Jacket is embroidered with blanket stich (see diagram)

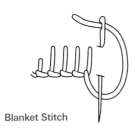

Blanket Stitch

CABLE PANEL CHARTS

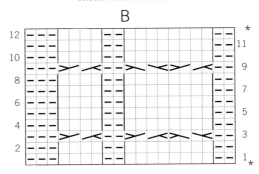

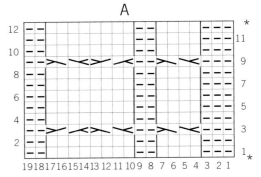

Repeat from * to *

☐ K on RS, p on WS

– P on RS, k on WS

Sl 2 sts on cable needle and hold in back, k2, then k2 from cable needle

Sl 2 sts on cable needle and hold in front, k2, then k2 from cable needle

40 - *Hooded Jacket* (continued)

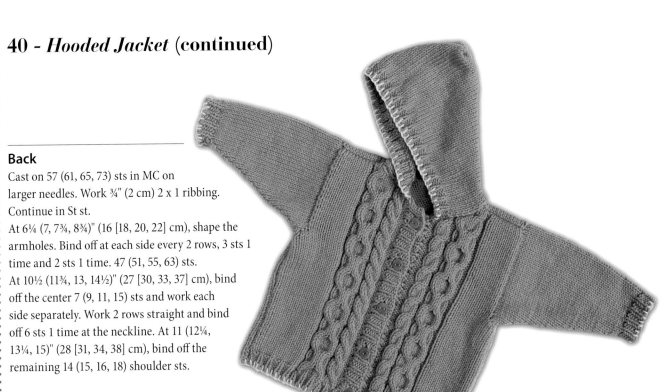

Back

Cast on 57 (61, 65, 73) sts in MC on larger needles. Work ¾" (2 cm) 2 x 1 ribbing. Continue in St st.

At 6¼ (7, 7¾, 8¾)" (16 [18, 20, 22] cm), shape the armholes. Bind off at each side every 2 rows, 3 sts 1 time and 2 sts 1 time. 47 (51, 55, 63) sts.

At 10½ (11¾, 13, 14½)" (27 [30, 33, 37] cm), bind off the center 7 (9, 11, 15) sts and work each side separately. Work 2 rows straight and bind off 6 sts 1 time at the neckline. At 11 (12¼, 13¼, 15)" (28 [31, 34, 38] cm), bind off the remaining 14 (15, 16, 18) shoulder sts.

Right Front

Cast on 29 (31, 33, 37) sts with MC on larger needles. Work ¾" (2 cm) of 2 x 1 ribbing. Using charts on page 94, work each row follows: 19 sts chart A, 10 (12, 14, 18) St sts.

At 6¼ (7, 7¾, 8¾)" 16 (18, 20, 22) cm, bind off along the left armhole as for the back. 24 (26, 28, 32) sts.

At 9½ (10½, 11½, 13)" (24 [27, 29, 33] cm), to shape the neckline, bind off along the RS every 2 rows as follows: 5 (6, 7, 9) sts 1 time, 3 sts 1 time, 1 st 2 times.

At 11 (12¼, 13¼, 15)" (28 [31, 34, 38] cm), bind off the remaining 14 (15, 16, 18) shoulder sts.

Left Front

Work the same reversing shaping and following chart B.

Sleeves

Cast on 40 (42, 44, 48) sts with MC on smaller needles. Work ¾" (2 cm) 2 x 1 ribbing. Change to larger needles and work in St st, inc 1 st at each side of every 3 rows: 9 (10, 11, 13) times. 58 (62, 66, 74) sts.

At 5½ (6¼, 7½, 8¾)" (14 [16, 19, 22] cm), bind off at each side every 2 rows as follows: 3 sts 1 time and 2 sts 1 time. Bind off the remaining sts.

Hood

Cast on 82 (86, 90, 98) sts with MC on larger needles. Work ¾" (2 cm) 2 x 1 ribbing then change to St st.

At 4¼ (4¾, 5½, 6¼)" (11 [12, 14, 16] cm), bind off 12 sts at each side every 2 rows, 3 times. Bind off the remaining sts.

Finishing

Button Band: Pick up and k 48 (54, 58, 66) sts in MC with smaller needles, along the right front edge. Work ¾" (2 cm) 2 x 1 ribbing, working five 1 st buttonholes in the center row with the first buttonhole placed 3 sts below the neckline and the remaining spaced 9 (11, 12, 14) sts apart. Bind off. Work the same on the left front without buttonholes.

Sew the shoulders. Fold the hood and seam it. Seam to the neckline.

Seam the sleeves. Seam the sleeves and the sides.

Embroider the edge of the hood, cuffs and hem with blanket stitch in CC (*see diagram on page 94*), with the top of the sts on the k st 2 rows above the edge. Sew on the buttons.

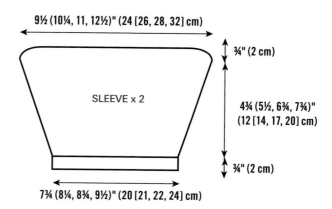

9½ (10¼, 11, 12½)" (24 [26, 28, 32] cm)

¾" (2 cm)

SLEEVE x 2

4¾ (5½, 6¾, 7¾)"
(12 [14, 17, 20] cm)

¾" (2 cm)

7¾ (8¼, 8¾, 9½)" (20 [21, 22, 24] cm)

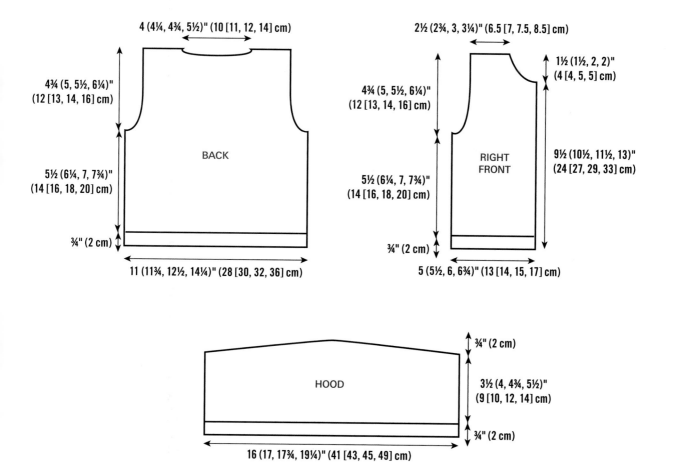

4 (4¼, 4¾, 5½)" (10 [11, 12, 14] cm)

4¾ (5, 5½, 6¼)"
(12 [13, 14, 16] cm)

BACK

5½ (6¼, 7, 7¾)"
(14 [16, 18, 20] cm)

¾" (2 cm)

11 (11¾, 12½, 14¼)" (28 [30, 32, 36] cm)

2½ (2¾, 3, 3¼)" (6.5 [7, 7.5, 8.5] cm)

1½ (1½, 2, 2)"
(4 [4, 5, 5] cm)

4¾ (5, 5½, 6¼)"
(12 [13, 14, 16] cm)

RIGHT
FRONT

9½ (10½, 11½, 13)"
(24 [27, 29, 33] cm)

5½ (6¼, 7, 7¾)"
(14 [16, 18, 20] cm)

¾" (2 cm)

5 (5½, 6, 6¾)" (13 [14, 15, 17] cm)

¾" (2 cm)

HOOD

3½ (4, 4¾, 5½)"
(9 [10, 12, 14] cm)

¾" (2 cm)

16 (17, 17¾, 19¼)" (41 [43, 45, 49] cm)

41 - *My First Scarf*

SIZE

- About 26" (66 cm) long

YARN

- Bulky weight (#5 Bulky)
  Phildar Partner 6 (50% polyamide, 25% wool, 25% acrylic; 71 yds [65 m]/1.76 oz [50 g]): Ecru (MC), 2 skeins; Ecru (CC), 1 skein

NEEDLES

- Size US 8 (5 mm)

NOTIONS

- Cable needle; tapestry needle

SPECIAL STITCHES

- **Cables A and B:** Work 8 sts of Chart A and B repeating the rows between * and *

Scarf

Cast on 26 sts in MC. Work 8 sts of chart A, 10 sts of 1 x 2 ribbing, 8 sts of chart B. At ¾" (2 cm), work St st on the center 10 sts.

At 25¼" (64 cm), work ¾" (2 cm) 1 x 2 ribbing on the 10 center sts and bind off. Embroider the ends with blanket stitch with CC (*see diagram on page 99*).

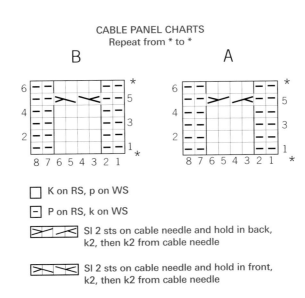

CABLE PANEL CHARTS
Repeat from * to *

B   A

☐ K on RS, p on WS

⊟ P on RS, k on WS

⟩⟨ Sl 2 sts on cable needle and hold in back, k2, then k2 from cable needle

⟩⟨ Sl 2 sts on cable needle and hold in front, k2, then k2 from cable needle

42 - Simple Cap with Earflaps

SIZE
• One size

YARN
• Bulky weight (#5 Bulky)
Phildar Partner 6 (50% polyamide, 25% wool, 25% acrylic; 71 yds [65 m]/1.76 oz [50 g]): Ecru (MC), and Naturel (CC), 1 skein each

NEEDLES
• Size US 8 (5 mm)

NOTIONS
• Tapestry needle

Bonnet

Cast on 5 sts MC. Work in St st. Inc 1 st each side every 2 rows 3 times. 11 sts. Put on hold and make the 2nd earflap the same.

Cast on 11 sts to make a half neck, and work across the 11 sts on one earflap, cast on 24 sts, k the 11 sts of the other earflap then cast on 11 sts for the other half neck. Work straight on the 68 sts for 4" (10 cm).

Shape the crown as follows: *5 sts, work 2tog, 6 sts, work 2tog, * 4 times, 5 sts, work 2tog, 1 st. 59 sts.

Work 3 rows straight, then on the next row: *4 sts, 2 sts tog, 5 st, 2 st tog* 4 times, 4 sts, 2 sts tog, 1 st. 50 sts.

Work 3 rows straight then on the next row: *3 st, 2 st tog, 4 st, 2 st tog *4 times, 3 st, 2 sts tog, 1 st. 41 sts.

Work 1 row then on the next row: *2 sts, 2 sts tog, 3 sts, 2 sts tog *4 times, 2 sts, 2 st tog, 1 st. 32 sts.

Work 1 row straight then on the next row: *1 st, 2 st tog, 2 sts, 2 sts tog *4 times, 1 st, 2 sts tog, 1 st. 23 sts.

Work 1 row straight then on the next row work 2 sts tog 11 times, 1 st. Work 1 row on 12 sts then on next row work 2 sts tog 6 times. Pass the yarn through the remaining 6 sts and pull tight and fasten the yarn. Seam the bonnet. Embroider blanket stitch (*see diagram to the right*) in CC around the edge of the bonnet. Attach a cord and tassel at the bottom of each earflap.

43 - Tasseled Mittens

SIZE
• One size

YARN
• Bulky weight (#5 Bulky)
Phildar Partner 6 (50% polyamide, 25% wool, 25% acrylic; 71 yds [65 m]/1.76 oz [50 g]): Ecru (MC), and Naturel (CC), 1 skein each

NEEDLES
• Size US 8 (5 mm)

NOTIONS
• Tapestry needle

Mittens

Cast on 9 sts in MC. Work ¾" (2 cm) 2 x 1 ribbing, then change to St st. Inc 1 st at each side every 2 rows 2 times. 13 sts.

At 2¾" (7 cm), dec 1 st at each side every 2 rows 2 times.

At 3¾" (9.5 cm), bind off the remaining sts.

Work the other side the same and place RS tog and seam around. Work the second mitten and join with a 27½" (70 cm) twisted cord in MC.

Embroider blanket stitch (*see diagram to the right*) with CC around each cuff with each point rows high and 1 st apart.

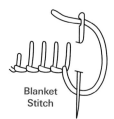

Blanket Stitch

44 - Beary Sweet Cardigan

Yarn: Sport weight (#2 Fine)

Sizes: 6 months (12 months, 24 months)

Needles: Size US 1 (2.5 mm) and Size US 2 (3 mm)

Un-Bear-ably Cut

46 – Grandpa Cardigan

Yarn: Sport weight (#2 Fine)
Sizes: 3 months (6 months, 12 months)
Needles: Size US 1 (2.5 mm) and Size US 2 (3 mm)

45 – Bear Paw Booties

Yarn: Sport weight (#2 Fine)
Size: 6 months
Needles: Size US 1 (2.5 mm) and Size US 2 (3 mm)

47 – Little Man Pants

Yarn: Fingering weight (#1 Super Fine)
Sizes: 3 months (6 months, 12 months)
Needles: Size US 1 (2.5 mm) and Size US 2 (3 mm)

44 - *Beary Cute Cardigan*

Is there anything cuter than a cuddly teddy bear? Your bab will be in this colorwork cardi. Match the bear's sweater in the colorwork pattern to your baby's, or mix it up and make a parade of rainbow bears!

SIZES

• 6 months (12 months, 24 months)

YARN

• Sport weight (#2 Fine)
  Phildar Lambswool (51% wool, 49% acrylic; 147 yds [134 m]/1.76 oz [50 g]): Azur (MC), 2 (3, 4) skeins; Blanc (CC1), and Chanvre (CC2), Café (CC3) 1 skein each

NEEDLES

• Size US 1 (2.5 mm) and Size US 2 (3 mm)
  Adjust needle size if necessary to obtain the correct gauge.

NOTIONS

• Five buttons; tapestry needle

GAUGE

• 26 sts and 36 rows = 4" (10 cm) in St st on larger needles

NOTES

• St st in colorwork follows the Bear Colorwork Chart being sure to twist the yarns when changing color

Back

Cast on 73 (79, 89) sts with MC on smaller needles Work ¾" (2 cm) 1 x 1 ribbing. Change to larger needles and work 27 rows of the Bear Colorwork Chart in St st starting with the 7th (4th, 13th) st. When the chart is worked, change to MC.
At 5½ (6¼, 7)" (14 [16, 18] cm), shape the armholes, binding off at each side every 2 rows: 3 sts 1 time, 2 sts, 1 time and 2 sts 1 time. 57 (63, 73) sts.
At 10¼ (11½, 13)" (26 [29, 33] cm), bind off the center 15 (17, 21) sts and work each side separately. Work 2 rows then bind off 6 st at the neckline. At 10½ (11¾, 13¼)" (27 [30, 34] cm), bind off the remaining 15 (17, 20) shoulder sts.

BEAR COLORWORK CHART

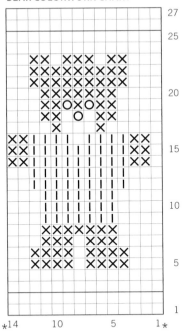

Repeat from * to *

☐ CC1
☒ CC2
☐ MC
⊙ CC3 (cross-stitch eyes)

Left Front

Cast on 37 (40, 45) sts with MC on smaller needles. Work ¾" (2 cm) 1 x 1 ribbing. Change to larger needles and work in St st as for the back starting at the same st on the chart. At 5½ (6¼, 7)" (14 [16, 18] cm), bind off along the right armhole as for the back. 29 (32, 37) sts. At 8¾ (9¾, 11½)" (22 [25, 29] cm), shape the neckline by binding off at the left side every 2 rows:

6 months: 6 sts, 3 sts, 2 sts, 1 st 2 times, work 4 rows then bind off 1 st.

12 months: 7 sts, 3 sts, 2 sts, 1 st 2 times then work 4 rows and bind off 1 st.

24 months: 7 sts, 3 sts, 2 sts 2 times, 1 st 2 times, work 4 rows and bind off 1 st.

At 27 (30, 34) cm, bind off all 15 (17, 20) sts.

Right Front

Work the same, reversing the shaping.

Sleeves

Cast on 45 (49, 53) sts with MC on smaller needles. Work ¾" (2 cm) 1 x 1 ribbing. With larger needles, work in St st as for the back starting with the 7th (5th, 3rd) st on the chart. Inc 1 st at each side: every 3 rows times (every 4 rows 14 times, every 4 rows 17 times). 71 (77, 87) sts.

At 6¼ (7½, 8¾)" (16 [19, 22] cm), bind off at each side every 2 rows: 3 sts, 2 sts, then 1 st 3 times. Bind off the rest.

Finishing

Embroider the eyes of the bears with cross-stitch. Sew the shoulders.

Neckline Border: Pick up and k 77 (83, 93) sts with MC on smaller needles. Work ¾" (2 cm) of 1 x 1 ribbing and bind off.

Button Bands: Pick up and k 69 (75, 85) sts with MC on smaller needles. Work ¾" (2 cm) of 1 x 1 ribbing and bind off. Work 5, 1 st buttonholes on one of the bands in the center row, the first 3 sts from one edge and the rest spaced on alternate 14 and 15 sts (16 sts, alternate 18 and 19 sts).

Seam the sleeves in the armholes and then seam the sleeves and sides. Sew on the buttons.

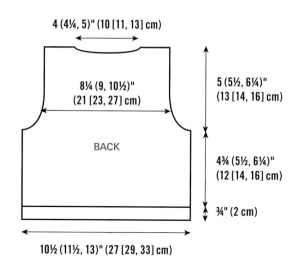

4 (4¼, 5)" (10 [11, 13] cm)

8¼ (9, 10½)" (21 [23, 27] cm)

5 (5½, 6¼)" (13 [14, 16] cm)

BACK

4¾ (5½, 6¼)" (12 [14, 16] cm)

¾" (2 cm)

10½ (11½, 13)" (27 [29, 33] cm)

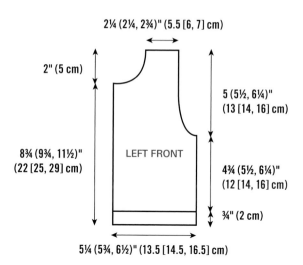

2¼ (2¼, 2¾)" (5.5 [6, 7] cm)

2" (5 cm)

5 (5½, 6¼)" (13 [14, 16] cm)

8¾ (9¾, 11½)" (22 [25, 29] cm)

LEFT FRONT

4¾ (5½, 6¼)" (12 [14, 16] cm)

¾" (2 cm)

5¼ (5¾, 6½)" (13.5 [14.5, 16.5] cm)

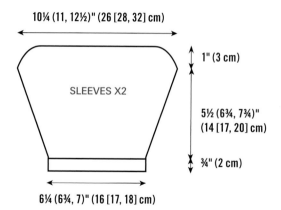

10¼ (11, 12½)" (26 [28, 32] cm)

1" (3 cm)

SLEEVES X2

5½ (6¾, 7¾)" (14 [17, 20] cm)

¾" (2 cm)

6¼ (6¾, 7)" (16 [17, 18] cm)

45 - *Bear Paw Booties*

Get a giggle out of these cute booties when baby's kicks reveal a bear on the bottom!

SIZE
- 3 to 6 months

YARN
- Sport weight (#2 Fine)
  Phildar Lambswool (51% wool, 49% acrylic; 147 yds [134 m]/1.76 oz [50 g]): Azur (MC), Blanc (CC1), and Chanvre (CC2), Café (CC3), 1 skein each

NEEDLES
- Size US 1 (2.5 mm) and Size US 2 (3 mm)

NOTIONS
- Tapestry needle

Sole
Cast on 7 sts in CC1 with larger needles. Work in St st. Inc 1 st at each side every row 2 times then every 2 rows 2 times. 15 sts. **AT THE SAME TIME**, starting on row 5 work a bear in the middle of the sole following the Bear Colorwork Chart, then end with CC1. Starting on row 25, dec 1 st on each side every 2 rows 3 times then dec 1 st on the next row. Bind off the remaining 7 sts on row 31.

Side of Foot
Cast on 64 sts in CC2 on larger needles. K 1 row on the WS then continue in St st in MC. Bind off on row 12 of St st.

Top of Foot
Cast on 14 sts in MC on larger needles. Work in St st. On row 11, dec 1 st each side every 2 rows 2 times, then 1 st every row 3 times. Bind off the 4 remaining sts on row 18.
Sew the side to the sole without seeming the back heel seam. Seam the top to the side.

Cuff
Pick up and k 42 sts in MC on smaller needles along the opening. Work 30 rows of 1 x 1 ribbing and bind off. Seam the back edges. Embroider the eyes.

BEAR COLORWORK CHART

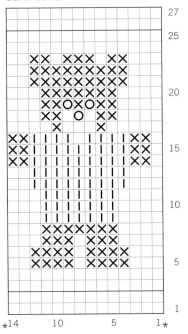

Repeat from * to *

- ☐ CC1
- ☒ CC2
- ⊺ MC
- ⊙ CC3 (cross-stitch eyes)

46 - *Grandpa Cardigan*

Knit a sweater with the look of a traditional V-neck cardigan in a pint size.
Whether you make it for a boy or a girl, it's a classic design that never gets old.

SIZES

- 3 months (6 months, 12 months)

YARN

- Sport weight (#2 Fine)
  Phildar Lambswool (51% wool, 49% acrylic; 147 yds
  [134 m]/1.76 oz [50 g]): Azur, 4 (4, 5) skeins

NEEDLES

- Size US 1 (2.5 mm) and Size US 2 (3 mm)
  *Adjust needle size if necessary to obtain the
  correct gauge.*

NOTIONS

- Cable needle; four buttons; tapestry needle

GAUGE

- 36 sts and 41 rows = 4" (10 cm) in stitch pattern on
  larger needles

SPECIAL STITCHES

- **Stitch Pattern:** Follow the Cable Stitch Chart
  repeating the 13 sts and 4 rows between the * and *.

Back

Cast on 87 (91, 103) sts on smaller needles. Work ¾" (2 cm) 1 x 1
ribbing, then p one row, inc 9 sts evenly. 96 (100, 112) sts.
Change to stitch pattern with larger needles starting with 1
edge sts, then st 13(11, 15) on the Cable Stitch Chart.
At 5 (6, 6¾)" (13 [15, 17] cm), shape the armholes. Bind off 5 (5,
6) sts at each side. 86 (90, 100) sts.
At 9¾ (11, 12¼)" (25 [28, 31] cm), bind off the center 6 (10, 14)
sts. Work each side separately and bind off at the shoulder edge
every 2 rows as follows:

3 months: 5 sts 3 times then 6 sts 2 times and at the neckline 5
sts 1 time and 4 sts 2 times.

6 months: 5 sts 3 times and 6 sts 2 times and at the neckline 5
sts 1 time and 4 sts 2 times.

12 months: 6 sts 5 times and at the neckline 5 sts 1 time and 4
sts 2 times.

CABLE STITCH CHART

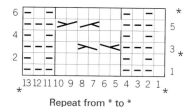

Repeat from * to *

☐	K on RS, p on WS
−	P on RS, k on WS

Sl 2 sts on cable needle and hold in back,
k2, then k2 from cable needle

Sl 2 sts on cable needle and hold in front,
k2, then k2 from cable needle

Work rows 1 to 6, then repeat rows 2 to 6. Repeat the sts
between * to *

46 - *Grandpa Cardigan* (continued)

Right Front

Cast on 41 (49, 49) sts on smaller needles. Work ¾" (2 cm) 1 x 1 ribbing, then p 1 row on the WS evenly making 4 inc. 45 (53, 53) sts. Work the Cable Stitch Chart (page 105) with larger needles starting with 1 edge st and st 12.

At 5 (6, 6¾)" (13 [15, 17] cm), shape the armhole binding off 5 (11, 6) sts at the left edge. 40 (42, 47) sts.

At 6¼ (7, 7¾)" (16 [18, 20] cm), shape the neckline binding off 1 st at the right edge then:

3 months: *1 st every 4 rows 1 time and 1 st every 2 rows 1 time* 4 times.

6 months: *1 st every 4 rows 1 time and 1 st every 2 rows 1 time* 6 times then 1 st every 4 rows 2 times.

12 months: *1 st every 4 rows 1 time, and 1 st every 2 rows 1 time * 8 times.

At 9¾ (11, 12¼)" (25 [28, 31] cm), bind off the shoulder as for the back.

Left Front

Work the same, reversing the shaping.

Sleeves

The sleeve is worked a bit short as the cables will naturally stretch vertically.

Cast on 48 (52, 56) sts on smaller needles. Work ¾" (2 cm) 1 x 1 ribbing then p 1 row on the WS evenly increasing 8 sts. 56 (60, 64) sts.

Work the Cable Stitch Chart with larger needles starting with 1 edge st, then st 7 (5, 3) on the chart.

Inc 1 st each side every 2 rows 3 times and every 4 rows 9 times (every 4 rows 13 times, every 4 rows 15 times). 80 (86, 94) sts.

At 6 (6¾, 7¾)" (15 [17.5, 20] cm) bind off loosely.

Finishing

Sew the shoulders.

Border: Pick up and k 193 (213, 238) sts on smaller needles along the fronts and back neckline. Work ¾" (2 cm) of 1 x 1 ribbing starting and ending with k2. In the center row make 4, 1 st buttonholes, the first 4 sts in from the bottom and remaining spaced 13 (15, 17) sts apart.

Seam sleeves to the armhole. Seam the sleeves and sides. Sew on buttons.

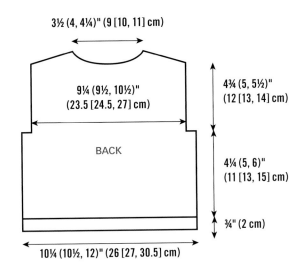

3½ (4, 4¼)" (9 [10, 11] cm)

9¼ (9½, 10½)" (23.5 [24.5, 27] cm)

4¾ (5, 5½)" (12 [13, 14] cm)

BACK

4¼ (5, 6)" (11 [13, 15] cm)

¾" (2 cm)

10¼ (10½, 12)" (26 [27, 30.5] cm)

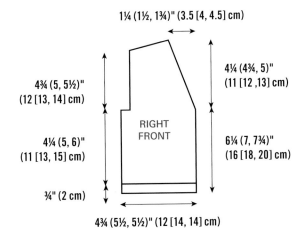

1¼ (1½, 1¾)" (3.5 [4, 4.5] cm)

4¾ (5, 5½)" (12 [13, 14] cm)

4¼ (4¾, 5)" (11 [12 ,13] cm)

RIGHT FRONT

4¼ (5, 6)" (11 [13, 15] cm)

6¼ (7, 7¾)" (16 [18, 20] cm)

¾" (2 cm)

4¾ (5½, 5½)" (12 [14, 14] cm)

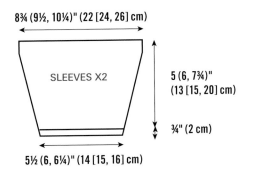

8¾ (9½, 10¼)" (22 [24, 26] cm)

SLEEVES X2

5 (6, 7¾)" (13 [15, 20] cm)

¾" (2 cm)

5½ (6, 6¼)" (14 [15, 16] cm)

47 - *Little Man Pants*

These lounge pants are great for your little man or little lady. The soft waistband ensures their tummy isn't pinched, while the tapered leg and cuff keeps them warm.

SIZES
- 3 months (6 months, 12 months)

YARN
- Sport weight (#2 Fine)
  Phildar Lambswool (51% wool, 49% acrylic; 147 yds [134 m]/1.76 oz [50 g]): Azur, 2 (3, 4) skeins

NEEDLES
- Size US 1 (2.5 mm) and Size US 2 (3 mm)
  Adjust needle size if necessary to obtain the correct gauge.

NOTIONS
- Elastic thread; tapestry needle

GAUGE
- 26 sts and 36 rows = 4" (10 cm) in St st on larger needles

NOTES
- Pants are worked in one piece, starting with the lower left leg

Back

Cast on 30 (33, 36) sts with smaller needles. Work ⅜" (1 cm) in 1 x 1 ribbing. Change to larger needles and St st. Inc 1 st at the right edge, every 5 (6, 7) rows 9 times. At 5½ (6¾, 7¾)" (14 [17, 20] cm) put the 39 (42, 45) sts on hold.

Work the right leg reversing shaping, then take up the left leg sts. 78 (84, 90) sts.

Shape the crotch by dec 1 st at each side of the 2 center sts 3 times every row then 1 st every other row 3 times. 66 (72, 78) sts.

At 11½ (13, 14½)" (29 [33, 37] cm), change to smaller needle and work 1" (3 cm) 1 x 1 ribbing. Bind off.

Front

Work as for the back.

Finishing

Sew the sides and the inner leg. Thread several rows of elastic thread under the waist ribbing.

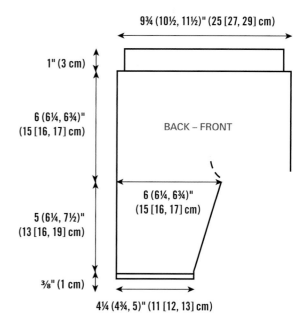

9¾ (10½, 11½)" (25 [27, 29] cm)

1" (3 cm)

6 (6¼, 6¾)" (15 [16, 17] cm)

BACK – FRONT

6 (6¼, 6¾)" (15 [16, 17] cm)

5 (6¼, 7½)" (13 [16, 19] cm)

⅜" (1 cm)

4¼ (4¾, 5)" (11 [12, 13] cm)

Nautical Newborns

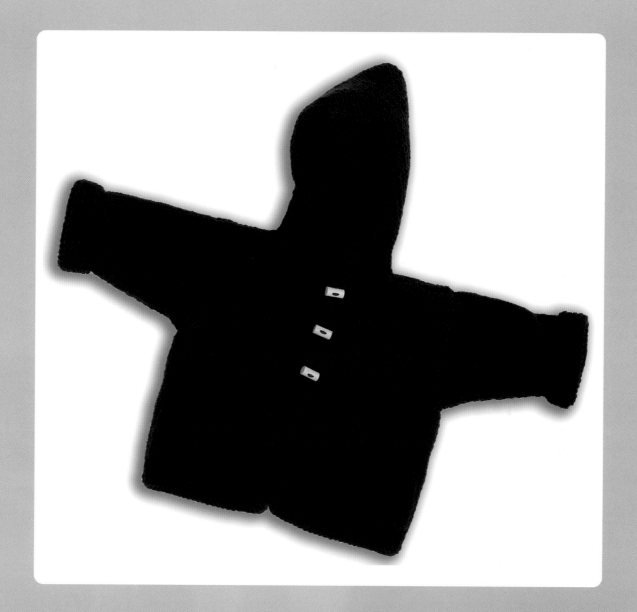

48 – Classic Peacoat with Toggles

Yarn: DK weight (#3 Light)

Sizes: 3 months (6 months, 12 months, 24 months)

Needles: Size US 6 (4 mm) and Size US 7 (4.5 mm)

48 - *Classic Peacoat with Toggles*

Keep the cold at bay with this traditional navy-inspired peacoat. The front closes easily with wood toggles and the hood provides an extra layer of warmth against sea winds.

SIZES

- 3 months (6 months, 12 months, 24 months)

YARN

- DK weight (#3 Light)
  Phildar Oxygène (40% acrylic, 35% chlorofiber, 25% combed wool; 148 yds [135 m]/1.76 oz [50 g]): Marine, 7 (8, 9, 10) skeins held double

NEEDLES

- Size US 6 (4 mm) and Size US 7 (4.5 mm)
  Adjust needle size if necessary to obtain the correct gauge.

NOTIONS

- Three wooden buttons; tapestry needle

GAUGE

- 17 sts and 22 rows = 4" (10 cm) in St st on larger needles with yarn held double

Back

Cast on 49 (53, 57, 65) sts with yarn held double on smaller needles. Work 4 rows in garter st. Change to larger needles and work in St st.

At 6¼ (7, 7¾, 8¾)" (16 [18, 20, 22] cm), change to garter st on smaller needles and shape the armholes, binding off each side every 2 rows: 2 sts 1 time and 1 st 1 time. 43 (47, 51, 59) sts. At 10½ (11¾, 13, 14½)" (27 [30, 33, 37] cm), bind off the center 15 (17, 19, 23) sts and work each side separately.

At 11 (12¼, 13¼, 15)" (28 [31, 34, 38] cm), bind off all 14 (15, 16, 18) shoulder sts.

Left Front

Cast on 29 (31, 33, 37) sts with the yarn held double on smaller needles. Work 4 rows in garter st. Change to larger needles and St st except on the last 4 sts which are always worked in garter to make the buttonhole band.

At 6 (6¾, 7½, 8¼)" (15 [17, 19, 21] cm), work a 1 st buttonhole 2 sts from the center front edge then work 2 other buttonholes spaced every 1½ (1¾, 1¾, 2¼)" (4 [4.5, 4.5, 5.5] cm).

At 6¼ (7, 7¾, 8¾)" (16 [18, 20, 22] cm), change to garter st on smaller needles and bind off along the right edge as for the back.

At 9½ (10½, 11½, 13)" (24 [27, 29, 33] cm), bind off along the left side every 2 rows to shape the neckline as follows: 5 (6, 7, 9) sts 1 time, 3 sts 1 time, then 1 st 2 times. At 11 (12¼, 13¼, 15)" (28 [31, 34, 38] cm), bind off all 14 (15, 16, 18) sts.

Right Front

Work the same reversing shaping omitting the buttonholes.

Sleeves

Cast on 33 (35, 37, 41) sts, with the yarn held double on smaller needles. Work 2" (5 cm) in garter st, then change to smaller needles and work in St st. Inc 1 st at each side every 5 rows: 5 (6, 7, 9) times. 43 (47, 51, 59) sts. At 7 (7¾, 9, 10¼)" (18 [20, 23, 26] cm), bind off at each side every 2 rows: 2 sts 1 time and 1 st 1 time. Bind off all.

Hood

Cast on 72 (76, 80, 88) sts with yarn held double on smaller needles. Work in garter st. At 5 (5½, 6¼, 7)" (13 [14, 16, 18] cm), bind off 15 sts each side every 2 rows 2 times. Bind off all.

Pockets

Cast on 20 sts with yarn held double on smaller needles. Work 3½" (9 cm) in garter st and bind off.

Finishing

Sew the shoulders. Fold the hood in half and seam the back. Seam the hood to the neckline attaching it from the beginning of the neckline border to the end of the other. Seam sleeves to the armhole. Seam the sides reversing the seam in the middle of the garter st. Sew the pockets to the fronts then sew on the buttons.

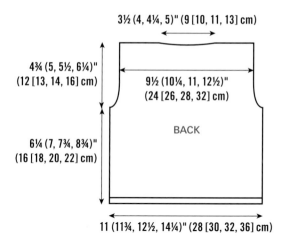

3½ (4, 4¼, 5)" (9 [10, 11, 13] cm)

4¾ (5, 5½, 6¼)" (12 [13, 14, 16] cm)

9½ (10¼, 11, 12½)" (24 [26, 28, 32] cm)

BACK

6¼ (7, 7¾, 8¾)" (16 [18, 20, 22] cm)

11 (11¾, 12½, 14¼)" (28 [30, 32, 36] cm)

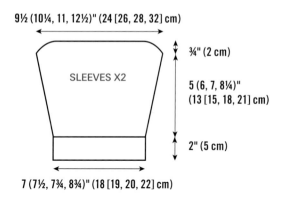

9½ (10¼, 11, 12½)" (24 [26, 28, 32] cm)

¾" (2 cm)

SLEEVES X2

5 (6, 7, 8¼)" (13 [15, 18, 21] cm)

2" (5 cm)

7 (7½, 7¾, 8¾)" (18 [19, 20, 22] cm)

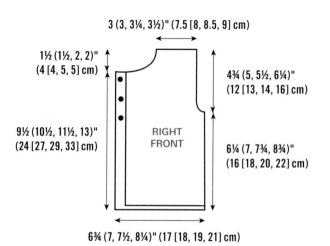

3 (3, 3¼, 3½)" (7.5 [8, 8.5, 9] cm)

1½ (1½, 2, 2)" (4 [4, 5, 5] cm)

4¾ (5, 5½, 6¼)" (12 [13, 14, 16] cm)

9½ (10½, 11½, 13)" (24 [27, 29, 33] cm)

RIGHT FRONT

6¼ (7, 7¾, 8¾)" (16 [18, 20, 22] cm)

6¾ (7, 7½, 8¼)" (17 [18, 19, 21] cm)

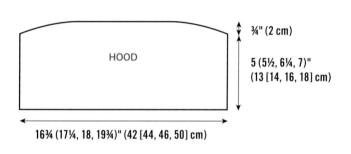

¾" (2 cm)

HOOD

5 (5½, 6¼, 7)" (13 [14, 16, 18] cm)

16¾ (17¼, 18, 19¾)" (42 [44, 46, 50] cm)

49 – Ocean Wave Socks

Yarn: Sport weight (#2 Fine)

Sizes: 3 months (6 months, 12 months)

Needles: Size US 2 (3 mm)

50 – Watch Cap

Yarn: DK weight (#3 Light)

Size: One size

Needles: Size US 6 (4 mm) and Size US 7 (4.5 mm)

51 – Tidal Currents Sweater

Yarn: Sport weight (#2 Fine)

Sizes: 3 months (6 months, 12 months)

Needles: Size US 1 (2.5 mm) and Size US 2 (3 mm)

52 – Button Front Sailor Pants

Yarn: Sport weight (#2 Fine)

Sizes: 3 months (6 months, 12 months)

Needles: Size US 1 (2.5 mm) and Size US 2 (3 mm)

49 - Ocean Waves Socks

Simple stripes added to a classic sock pattern give these wardrobe essentials a custom look.

SIZES
- 3 months (6 months, 12 months)

YARN
- Sport weight (#2 Fine)
  Phildar Lambswool (51% wool, 49% acrylic; 147 yds [134 m]/1.76 oz [50 g]): Indigo (MC), Blanc (CC), 1 skein each

NEEDLES
- Size US 2 (3 mm)
  Adjust needle size if necessary to obtain the correct gauge.

NOTIONS
- Tapestry needle

GAUGE
- 26 sts and 36 rows = 4" (10 cm) in St st

SPECIAL STITCHES
- **Skp:** Sl 1, k 1 pass slipped st over

Socks

Cast on 32 (36, 40) sts in MC. Work ⅜" (1 cm) 2 x 1 ribbing then change to St st alternating 2 rows CC with 4 rows MC.

After the 3rd (4th, 5th) stripe in MC, work the half heel on the first 8 sts in St st using CC. Shape the heel by leaving 1 more st on hold towards the center every 2 rows 5 times then working 1 more st every 2 rows 5 times. Work the same on the 8 sts at the other end. Change to MC and work the foot on all the sts.

When the foot is 1½ (1¾, 2)" (4 [4.5, 5] cm) long, change to CC and shape the toe as follows: work 6 (7, 8) sts, skp, k2tog, work 12 (14, 16) sts, skp, k2tog, work 6 (7, 8) sts. Repeat this shaping on the next row then on every other row 4 times, working the dec on top of each other. Thread the yarn through the remaining sts and pull tightly and fix the tail. Seam the sole and leg.

50 - *Watch Cap*

Knit a traditional watch cap with a fold-over brim for your wee seafarer's next beach adventure.

SIZE
• One size

YARN
• DK weight (#3 Light)
Phildar Oxygène (40% acrylic, 35% chlorofiber, 25% combed wool; 148 yds [135 m]/1.76 oz [50 g]): Marine, 1 skein

NEEDLES
• Size US 6 (4 mm) and Size US 7 (4.5 mm)

NOTIONS
• Tapestry needle

Cap

Cast on 58 sts holding the yarn double using smaller needles. Work 1½" (4 cm) of 2 x 2 ribbing then change to larger needles, and work in St st.
At 5" (13 cm), shape the crown: 1 edge st * k2tog, k 6* 7 times, 1 edge stitch.
Repeat this shaping with dec one over the other, every 2 rows. Thread the yarn through the remaining sts and pull tight and attach firmly. Seam the edge sts together.

51 - *Ocean Currents Sweater*

No nautical-themed wardrobe is complete without a classic striped top. This pullover is worked in pieces and then seamed after.

SIZES
- 3 months (6 months, 12 months)

YARN
- Sport weight (#2 Fine)
  Phildar Lambswool (51% wool, 49% acrylic; 147 yds [134 m]/1.76 oz [50 g]): Blanc (MC), 2 (3, 3) skeins; Indigo (CC), 1 skein

NEEDLES
- Size US 1 (2.5 mm) and Size US 2 (3 mm)
  Adjust needle size if necessary to obtain the correct gauge.

NOTIONS
- Four white buttons; tapestry needle

GAUGE
- 26 sts and 36 rows = 4" (10 cm) in St st on larger needles

Back

Cast on 59 (65, 71) sts in MC on larger needles. Work ⅜" (1 cm) 2 x 1 ribbing then change to St st working 2 rows in CC and 4 rows in MC. After the 7th (8th, 9th) CC stripe, change back to MC.

At 4¾ (5½, 6¼)" (12 [14, 16] cm), shape the armholes. Bind off at each side, every 2 rows: 2 sts 1 times then 1 st 3 times. 49 (55, 61) sts.

At 8 (9¼, 10½)" (20.5 [23.5, 26.5] cm), bind off all sts.

Front

Work as for the back.

At 6¾ (8, 9¼)" (17.5 [20.5, 23.5] cm), bind off the center 9 (11, 13) sts and work each side separately. Shape the neckline by binding off at the neckline every 2 rows as follows: 3 sts 1 time, then 2 sts 1 time, then 1 st 2 times.

At 8 (9¼, 10½)" (20.5 [23.5, 26.5] cm), bind off the remaining 13 (15, 17) shoulder sts.

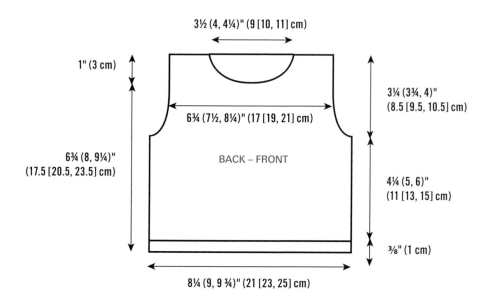

3½ (4, 4¼)" (9 [10, 11] cm)

1" (3 cm)

3¼ (3¾, 4)" (8.5 [9.5, 10.5] cm)

6¾ (7½, 8¼)" (17 [19, 21] cm)

6¾ (8, 9¼)" (17.5 [20.5, 23.5] cm)

BACK – FRONT

4¼ (5, 6)" (11 [13, 15] cm)

⅜" (1 cm)

8¼ (9, 9 ¾)" (21 [23, 25] cm)

Sleeves

Cast on 38 (41, 44) sts in MC on smaller needles. Work ⅜" (1 cm) 2 x 1 ribbing then change to St st working as for the back, evenly inc 0 (1, 2) sts on row 1 then inc 1 st at each side:

3 months: Every 7 rows 5 times. 48 sts.
6 months: Every 7 rows 6 times. 54 sts.
12 months: Every 8 rows 7 times. 60 sts.
At 4¼ (5, 6¾)" (11 [13, 17] cm), bind off at each side, every 2 rows 2 sts 1 time and 3 times 1 time. Bind off the rest.

Finishing

Back Border: Pick up and k 48 (54, 60) sts in MC using smaller needles along the top of the back. Work ⅜" (1 cm) 2 x 1 ribbing and bind off.
Front Border Buttonhole Band: Pick up and k 54 (60, 66) sts along the shoulders and neckline and work as for the back but make 1 st buttonhole on row 1, 2 sts in from the shoulder and 1 st in from the neckline along both shoulders.
Sew on buttons. Seam sleeves to the armhole sewing through both layers of the borders. Seam the sleeves and sides.

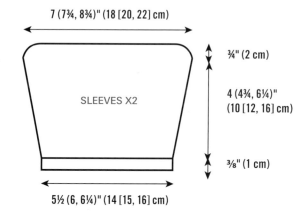

7 (7¾, 8¾)" (18 [20, 22] cm)

¾" (2 cm)

SLEEVES X2

4 (4¾, 6¼)" (10 [12, 16] cm)

⅜" (1 cm)

5½ (6, 6¼)" (14 [15, 16] cm)

52 - *Button Front Sailor Pants*

These cute bottoms have a fun vintage feel. The button front is reminiscent of 1940s style while allowing quick access for diaper changing.

SIZES
- 3 months (6 months, 12 months)

YARN
- Sport weight (#2 Fine)
  Phildar Lambswool (51% wool, 49% acrylic; 147 yds [134 m]/1.76 oz [50 g]): Indigo, 2(3, 3) skeins

NEEDLES
- Size US 1 (2.5 mm) and Size US 2 (3 mm)
  Adjust needle size if necessary to obtain the correct gauge.

NOTIONS
- Four white buttons; elastic thread; tapestry needle

GAUGE
- 26 sts and 36 rows = 4" (10 cm) in St st on larger needles

NOTES
- Pants are worked in two pieces and seamed, starting at the lower left leg

Back

Cast on 31 (34, 37) sts on larger needles. Work ⅜" (1 cm) 2 x 1 ribbing, then change to St st inc 1 st at the right edge every: 5 (6, 7) rows 9 times. 40 (43, 46) sts. At 5½ (6¾, 7¾)" (14 [17, 20] cm) put the sts on hold. Work the right leg reversing the shaping then take up the left leg sts. 80 (86, 92) sts. Work crotch shaping by dec 1 st at each side of the center 2 sts each row 3 times then every 2 rows 3 times. 68 (74, 80) sts. At 11 (12½, 14¼)" (28 [32, 36] cm), change to smaller needles and work 1" (3 cm) of 1 x 1 ribbing. Bind off.

Front

Work as for the back. At 8¾ (10¼, 11¾)" (22 [26, 30] cm), make the front panel by working only on the center 30 (32, 34) sts for 3" (8 cm) in St st, then ⅜" (1 cm) 2 x 1 ribbing. Bind off. Working the side sts on hold separately, with 2¼" (6 cm) of St st then 1" (3 cm) of 1 x 1 ribbing. Bind off.

Finishing

Center Front Panel Border: Pick up and k 23 sts along each side of the front panel. Work ⅜" (1 cm) 2 x 1 ribbing and bind off.

Sew the ribbing at the sides of the panel to the edge of the side fronts. Sew the sides and inseam. Thread several rows of elastic thread through the ribbing along the waist. Sew the decorative buttons along the panel border.

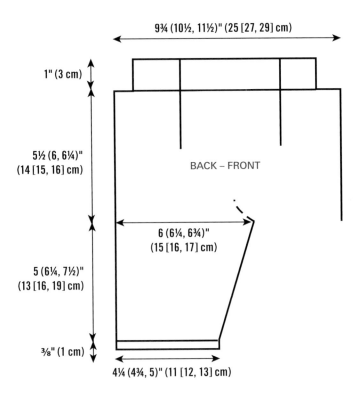

9¾ (10½, 11½)" (25 [27, 29] cm)

1" (3 cm)

5½ (6, 6¼)" (14 [15, 16] cm)

BACK – FRONT

6 (6¼, 6¾)" (15 [16, 17] cm)

5 (6¼, 7½)" (13 [16, 19] cm)

⅜" (1 cm)

4¼ (4¾, 5)" (11 [12, 13] cm)

53 – Elvish Cabled Sack

Yarn: Aran weight (#4 Medium)

Size: Newborn to 3 months

Needles: Size US 7 (4.5 mm) and Size US 8 (5 mm)

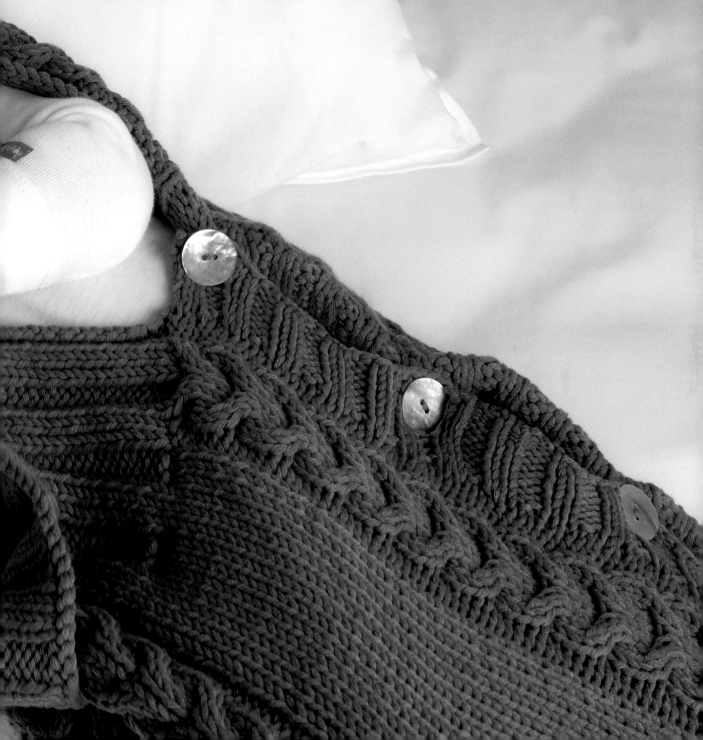

Adorable Must-Makes

53 - *Elvish Cabled Sack*

Snuggle your precious little one up in this cocoon fit for fairy-tale dreams. Classic cabling pairs with a stately tasseled hood and buttoned sides mean you can tuck a sleeping baby in with ease.

SIZE
- Newborn to 3 months

YARN
- Aran weight (#4 Medium)
  Phildar Avisol (60% cotton, 40% acrylic; 74 yds [68 m]/1.76 oz [50 g]): Romarin, 7 skeins

NEEDLES
- Size US 7 (4.5 mm) and Size US 8 (5 mm)
  Adjust needle size if necessary to obtain the correct gauge.

NOTIONS
- Cable needle; stitch markers; eight large buttons; tapestry needle

GAUGE
- 17 sts and 22 rows = 4" (10 cm) in St st on larger needles

SPECIAL STITCHES
- **Cable Pattern:** (12 st, 6 row repeat)
  Row 1: P2, k8, p2.
  Rows 2, 4, 6: Work the sts as they present.
  Row 3: P2, put 2 sts on cable needle and hold in back. K2, then k2 from cable needle, p2.
  Row 5: work as for row 1.
  Repeat Rows 1–6.

Front
Cast on 64 sts on larger needles. Work 1 edge st *12 st cable pattern, 13 St sts * 2 times, 12 st cable, 1 edge st. At 15¾" (40 cm), change to 3 x 3 ribbing dec 1 st in the middle of row 1. When there is 4" (10 cm) of ribbing, bind off.

Back
Cast on 71 sts on larger needles. Work 1 edge st, 12 sts cable, 45 sts 3 x 3 ribbing, 12 sts cable pattern, 1 edge sts. At 26" (66 cm) bind off.

Finishing
Place a marker 15¾" (40 cm) up from the cast on edge at each side of the back and front. Place the front along the back matching the markers and seam the cast on edges together.
Button Bands: Pick up and k 120 sts along the front and back sides between the markers using smaller needles. Work 1" (3 cm) of 2 x 2 ribbing starting and ending with k3. Make 4, 2 st buttonholes in the center row—the first, 1" (3 cm) from the top front marker and the rest spaced 12 sts apart. Bind off.
Hood: Join the 2 parts marked A and seam.
Hood Border: Pick up and k 100 sts along the edge of the hood. K 1 row on the WS then bind off.
Lay the cocoon flat with the button bands WS together and sew buttons on the back border.
Make a tassel and fix to the point of the hood.

CABLE PANEL CHART

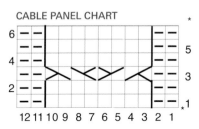

Repeat from * to *

☐ = K on RS, p on WS

⊟ = P on RS, k on WS

 = Sl 2 sts on cable needle and hold in front, k2, then k2 from cable needle

 = Sl 2 sts on cable needle and hold in back, k2, then k2 from cable

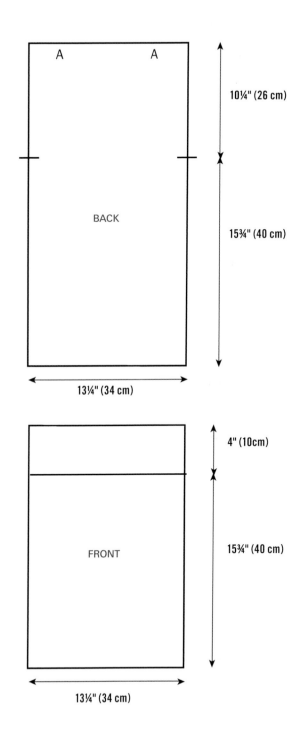

A   A

10¼" (26 cm)

BACK

15¾" (40 cm)

13¼" (34 cm)

4" (10cm)

FRONT

15¾" (40 cm)

13¼" (34 cm)

54 – Pixie Hat

Yarn: Sport weight (#2 Fine)
Sizes: 3 months (6 months, 12 months)
Needles: Size US 2 (3 mm)

55 & 56 – Simple Wide Leg Pants and Frog Button Coat

Yarn: Sport weight (#2 Fine)

Sizes: 3 months (6 months, 12 months)

Needles: Size US 1 (2.5 mm) and Size US 2 (3 mm)

54 - *Pixie Hat*

This cute little hat works up quick as can be, making for an easy accessory that you'll want to make in every color.

SIZES
- 3 months (6 months, 12 months)

YARN
- Sport weight (#2 Fine)
  Phildar Lambswool (51% wool, 49% acrylic; 147 yds [134 m]/1.76 oz [50 g]): Noir, 1 skein

NEEDLES
- Size US 2 (3 mm)
  Adjust needle size if necessary to obtain the correct gauge.

NOTIONS
- Cable needle; tapestry needle

GAUGE
- 26 sts and 35 rows = 4" (10 cm) in St st

SPECIAL STITCHES
- **Double dec:** Put 2 sts on cable needle and hold in front. Work the first st on the cable needle together with the first st on the left needle. Repeat with the second st.

Bonnet

Cast on 94 (102, 110) sts. Work 4 rows in garter st, then change to St st. At 2¼ (2¾, 3)" (6 [7, 8] cm) long, shape the top as follows: 1 edge st, 10 (11, 12) sts, *1 double dec (*see Special Stitches*), 20 (22, 24) sts * 3 times, 1 double dec, 10 (11, 12) sts, 1 edge stitch. Repeat working the dec above each other every 2 rows, 4 (5, 6) more times, then every row 5 times. 14 sts. K2 tog across and then work 2¾" (7 cm) on the remaining 7 sts. Thread the yarn through all the sts, pull tightly and fix seam.

55 - *Simple Wide Leg Pants*

You can never have too many wardrobe staples, such as these simple wide-legged pants. Knit them up in the same color as the Frog Button Cardigan for a matching ensemble, or mix and match your favorite colors!

SIZES
- 3 months (6 months, 12 months)

YARN
- Sport weight (#2 Fine)
  Phildar Lambswool (51% wool, 49% acrylic; 147 yds [134 m]/1.76 oz [50 g]): Indigo, 2 (2, 3) skeins

NEEDLES
- Size US 1 (2.5 mm) and Size US 2 (3 mm)
  Adjust needle size if necessary to obtain the correct gauge.

NOTIONS
- Elastic thread; tapestry needle

GAUGE
- 26 sts and 35 rows = 4" (10 cm) in St st on larger needles

NOTES
- Pants are worked in two pieces, and seamed starting at the lower left leg

SPECIAL STITCHES
- **Skp:** Sl 1, k1, pass slipped st over

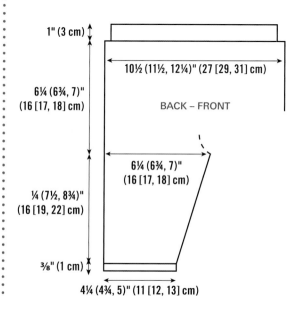

1" (3 cm)

10½ (11½, 12¼)" (27 [29, 31] cm)

6¼ (6¾, 7)" (16 [17, 18] cm)

BACK – FRONT

6¼ (6¾, 7)" (16 [17, 18] cm)

¼ (7½, 8¾)" (16 [19, 22] cm)

⅜" (1 cm)

4¼ (4¾, 5)" (11 [12, 13] cm)

Back
Cast on 30 (33, 36) sts on larger needles. Work 4 rows of garter st then change to St st. Inc 1 st along the right edge every 6 rows 4 times, then every 4 rows 8 times (alternate dec at 6 rows then 4 rows 12 times, every 6 rows 12 times).
At 6¾ (7¾, 9)" (17 [20, 23] cm), put the 42 (45, 48) sts on hold. Work the right leg reversing shaping then take up the left leg sts. 84 (90, 96) sts. Shape the crotch by dec 1 st at each side the middle 2 sts every 2 rows 6 times as follows: skp, k2, k2tog. 72 (78, 84) sts.
At 13 (14½, 16)" (33 [37, 41] cm), change to smaller needles. Work 1" (3 cm) 1 x 1 ribbing. Bind off.

Front
Work as for the back.

Finishing
Sew the sides and the inseam. Thread several rows of elastic thread under the waistband ribbing.

56 - *Frog Button Coat*

Wrap baby up snug as can be in this stylish knitted coat. The looping embroidered embellishments mimic vintage frog buttons.

SIZES
- 3 months (6 months, 12 months)

YARN
- Sport weight (#2 Fine)
  Phildar Lambswool (51% wool, 49% acrylic; 147 yds [134 m]/1.76 oz [50 g]): Indigo, 2 (2, 3) skeins

NEEDLES
- Size US 1 (2.5 mm) and Size US 2 (3 mm)
  Adjust needle size if necessary to obtain the correct gauge.

NOTIONS
- Three garment snaps; elastic thread; tapestry needle

GAUGE
- 26 sts and 35 rows = 4" (10 cm) in St st on larger needles

NOTES
- The frogs are embroidered with chain st

Back

Cast on 78 (84, 90) sts on larger needles. Work 4 rows of garter st then change to St st and dec 1 st at each side every 20 rows 2 times. 74 (80, 86) sts.
At 6 (6¾, 7½)" (15 [17, 19] cm), shape the armholes by binding off at each side, every 2 rows: 3 sts 1 time, 2 sts 1 time, and 1 st 2 times. 60 (66, 72) sts. At 10½ (11¾, 13)" (27 [30, 33] cm), bind off the center 14 (16, 18) sts and work each side separately. Work 2 rows straight then bind off 6 sts at the neckline.
At 11 (12¼, 13¼)" (28 [31, 34] cm), bind off the remaining 17 (19, 21) shoulder sts.

Right Front

Cast on 39 (42, 45) sts on larger needles. Work 4 rows in garter st then change to St st working the dec as for the back along the left edge. 37 (40, 43) sts.
At 6 (6¾, 7½)" (15 [17, 19] cm), work the armhole shaping along the left side as for the back. 30 (33, 36) sts. At 9½ (10½, 11½)" (24 [27, 29] cm) shape the neckline by binding off at the RS every 2 rows: 5 (6, 7) sts 1 time, 3 sts 1 time, 2 sts 1 time, and 1 st 3 times. At 11 (12¼, 13¼)" (28 [31, 34] cm) bind off the remaining 17 (19, 21) sts.

Left Front

Work the same, reversing the shaping.

Sleeves

Cast on 43 (46, 49) sts on larger needles. Work 4 rows in garter st, then change to St st and inc 1 st at each end as follows:

3 months: Every 4 rows 6 times, then alternate every 2 and 4 rows 7 times. 69 sts.

6 months: Every 4 rows 14 times. 74 sts.

12 months: Every 4 rows 15 times. 79 sts.

At 6 (6¾, 7¾)" (15 [17, 20] cm), bind off every 2 rows at each side: 1 st 2 times, 2 sts 1 time, then 3 sts 1 time.

Bind off the remaining sts.

Collar

Cast on 64 (70, 76) sts smaller needles. Work 8 rows in St st. Put on hold. Pick up and k 6 st along the edge then work 3 rows of garter st on all 76 (82, 88) sts. Bind off loosely.

Finishing

Front Borders: Pick up and k 59 (66, 71) sts on smaller needles at the edge of each front. Work 3 rows in garter st and bind off. Sew the shoulders. Seam sleeves to the armhole. Seam the sleeves and sides. Seam the collar to the neckline leaving the borders free.

Embroider 3 frogs spaced on each front (see frog diagram). Sew the snaps to the front borders.

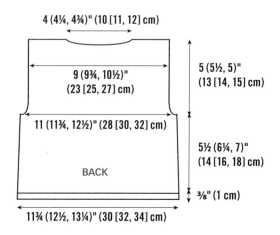

4 (4¼, 4¾)" (10 [11, 12] cm)

9 (9¾, 10½)" (23 [25, 27] cm)

5 (5½, 5)" (13 [14, 15] cm)

11 (11¾, 12½)" (28 [30, 32] cm)

BACK

5½ (6¼, 7)" (14 [16, 18] cm)

⅜" (1 cm)

11¾ (12½, 13¼)" (30 [32, 34] cm)

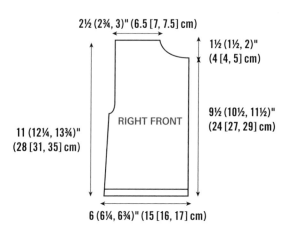

2½ (2¾, 3)" (6.5 [7, 7.5] cm)

1½ (1½, 2)" (4 [4, 5] cm)

11 (12¼, 13¾)" (28 [31, 35] cm)

RIGHT FRONT

9½ (10½, 11½)" (24 [27, 29] cm)

6 (6¼, 6¾)" (15 [16, 17] cm)

FROGS
Enlarge to 125%

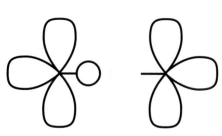

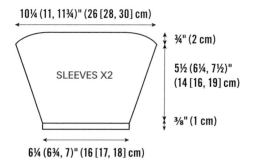

10¼ (11, 11¾)" (26 [28, 30] cm)

¾" (2 cm)

SLEEVES X2

5½ (6¼, 7½)" (14 [16, 19] cm)

⅜" (1 cm)

6¼ (6¾, 7)" (16 [17, 18] cm)

57 – Saddle Shoulder Pullover

Yarn: Sport weight (#2 Fine)

Sizes: 3 months (6 months, 12 months)

Needles: Size US 1 (2.5 mm) and Size US 2 (3 mm)

58 – Little Rider Leggings

Yarn: Sport weight (#2 Fine)

Sizes: 3 months (6 months, 12 months)

Needles: Size US 1 (2.5 mm) and Size US 2 (3 mm)

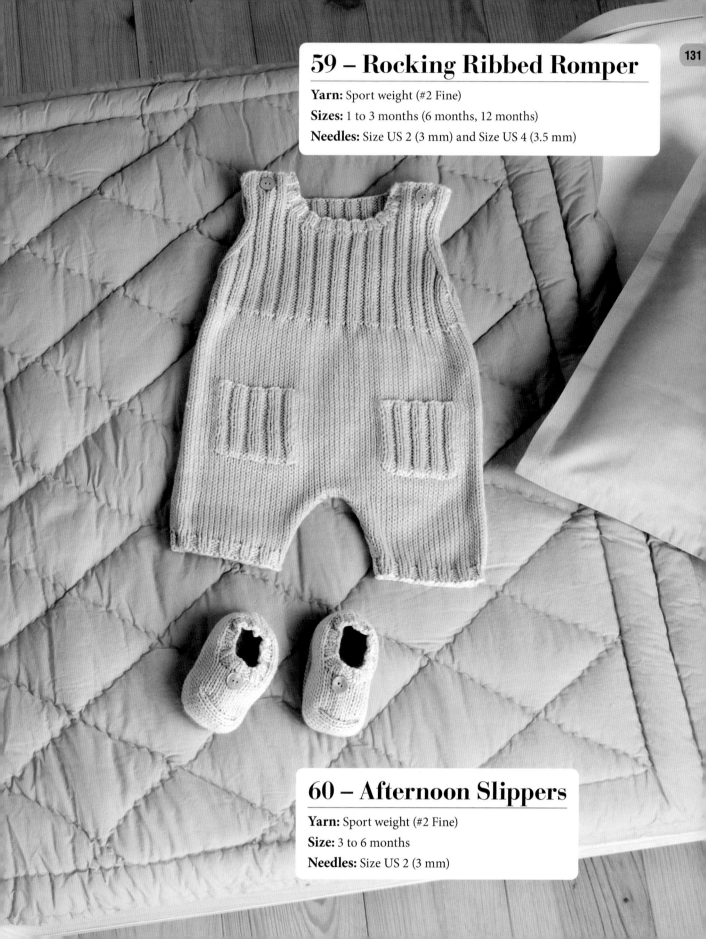

59 – Rocking Ribbed Romper

Yarn: Sport weight (#2 Fine)
Sizes: 1 to 3 months (6 months, 12 months)
Needles: Size US 2 (3 mm) and Size US 4 (3.5 mm)

60 – Afternoon Slippers

Yarn: Sport weight (#2 Fine)
Size: 3 to 6 months
Needles: Size US 2 (3 mm)

57 - Saddle Shoulder Pullover

Get ready to hop in the saddle with this stylish yet simple pullover. Buttoned saddle shoulders add a fun pop of color while also making for easy changing time.

SIZES

- 3 months (6 months, 12 months)

YARN

- Sport weight (#2 Fine)
  Phildar Phil Cotton 3 (100% cotton; 132 yds [121 m]/1.76 oz [50 g]): Perle (MC), 3 (3, 4) skeins; Mercure (CC), 1 skein

NEEDLES

- Size US 1 (2.5 mm) and Size US 2 (3 mm)
  Adjust needle size if necessary to obtain the correct gauge.

NOTIONS

- Four buttons; tapestry needle

GAUGE

- 26 sts and 36 rows = 4" (10 cm) in St st on larger needles

Back

Cast on 62 (66, 74) sts in MC, on larger needles. Work ¾" (2 cm) of 2 x 2 ribbing. Inc 0 (2, 0) sts evenly on last row. 62 (68, 74) sts. At 6 (6¾, 7½)" (15 [17, 19] cm), shape the armholes: bind off every 2 rows: 2 sts 2 times, 1 st 2 times. 50 (56, 62) sts. At 9½ (10¾, 12)" (24.5 [27.50, 30.5] cm), work 1 row of 2 x 2 ribbing starting and ending with k 2 (3, 2) on the RS. Continue in CC and work 1 row then on the next row bind off the center 20 (24, 26) sts. Work each side separately on 15 (16, 18) sts for 2¼" (6 cm) and bind off.

Front

Work as for the back until it is 7½ (8¾, 9¾)" (19 [22, 25] cm) long. Change to 2 x 2 ribbing starting and ending with k 2 (3, 2) on the RS. Work 4 rows MC, 1 row CC and bind off. **AT THE SAME TIME**, work 4, 1 st buttonholes on the 3rd row in MC: the first at 3 sts in from each end and the other 6 (8, 10) sts from the first.

Sleeves

Cast on 38 (42, 46) sts in CC with smaller needles. Work in 2 x 2 ribbing as follows: 1 row CC then change to MC for ¾" (2 cm). Change to larger needles and work in St st. Inc 1 st every 5 rows 8 times, (every 6 rows 9 times, every 6 rows 10 times). 54 (60, 66) sts.
At 6 (7, 7¾)" (15 [18, 20] cm), bind off at each side every 2 rows: 2 sts 2 times then 1 st 2 times. Bind off all.

Finishing

Sew on buttons ⅜" (1 cm) from top of the back straps. Button and sew the edges to keep in place. Seam sleeves to the armhole. Seam the sleeves and sides.

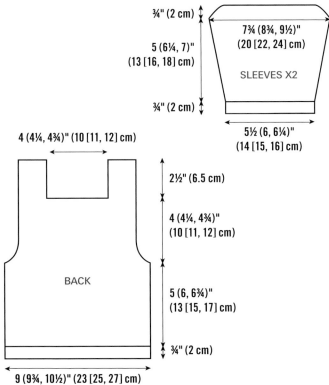

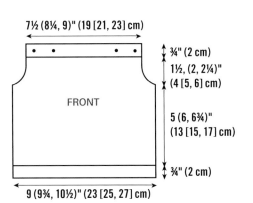

58 - *Little Rider Leggings*

This stylish pair of paints are perfect for your little rider. The buttoned opening also makes for easy changing.

SIZES
- 3 months (6 months, 12 months)

YARN
- Sport weight (#2 Fine)
  Phildar Phil Cotton 3 (100% cotton; 132 yds [121 m]/1.76 oz [50 g]): Perle (MC), 2 (2, 3) skeins; Mercure (CC), 1 skein

NEEDLES
- Size US 1 (2.5 mm) and Size US 2 (3 mm)
  Adjust needle size if necessary to obtain the correct gauge.

NOTIONS
- Elastic thread; three buttons; tapestry needle

GAUGE
- 26 sts and 36 rows = 4" (10 cm) in St st on larger needles

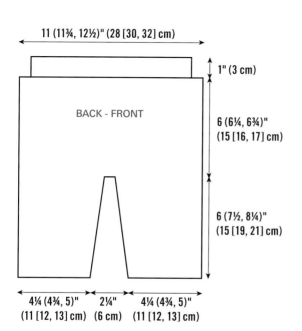

11 (11¾, 12½)" (28 [30, 32] cm)

1" (3 cm)

BACK - FRONT

6 (6¼, 6¾)" (15 [16, 17] cm)

6 (7½, 8¼)" (15 [19, 21] cm)

4¼ (4¾, 5)" (11 [12, 13] cm)   2¼" (6 cm)   4¼ (4¾, 5)" (11 [12, 13] cm)

Back
It is worked in one piece. Start at the lower left leg. Cast on 30 (33, 36) sts in CC on smaller needles. Work in 2 x 2 ribbing for 1 row then work 4 rows in MC. Change to larger needles and work in St st. Inc 1 st at each right edge every 6 (8, 9) rows 8 times. At 6 (7½, 8¼)" (15 [19, 21] cm), put the sts on hold.

Work the right leg reversing shaping then cast on 2 sts and work the left leg sts. 78 (84, 90) sts. At 11¾ (13¾, 15)" (30 [35, 38] cm), work 1" (3 cm) of 1 x 1 ribbing on smaller needles and bind off.

Front
Work as for the back.

False Fly Button Band: Cast on 32 sts in MC on larger needles. Work 4 rows of 2 x 2 ribbing starting and ending with k3. Bind off.

Finishing
Sew the sides then the inseam. Thread several rows of elastic thread under the waistband ribbing. Sew the false fly button band to the middle of the front and sew buttons on top.

59 - *Rocking Ribbed Romper*

SIZES

- 1 to 3 months (6 months, 12 months)

YARN

- Sport weight (#2 Fine)
  Phildar Phil Noé (50% cotton, 50% acrylic; 142 yds [130 m]/1.76 oz [50 g]): Ivory, 2 (3, 3) skeins

NEEDLES

- Size US 3 (3 mm) and Size US 4 (3.5 mm)
  Adjust needle size if necessary to obtain the correct gauge.

NOTIONS

- Two buttons; tapestry needle

GAUGE

- 22 sts and 32 rows = 4" (10 cm) in St st on larger needles

Front

Cast on 24 (26, 28) sts on smaller needles. Work ¾" (2 cm) in 2 x 2 ribbing. Change to larger needles and work in St st. Starting on row 4, inc 1 st at the right edge every 2 (3, 3) rows 5 times. At 1½, (2, 2¼)" (4 [5, 6] cm) put on hold.
Work the right leg reversing shaping. Cast on 3 sts for the crotch and take up the left leg sts. 61 (65, 69) sts.
At 9½ (10¾, 12)" (24.5 [27.5, 30.5] cm), change to smaller needles and work in 2 x 2 ribbing. In the middle of the last row inc 1 st. 62 (66, 70) sts.
At 10½ (11¾, 13)" (27 [30, 33] cm), cast on 2 st at each side and work the armhole shaping as follows: dec 1 st, 3 sts in from each edge every row 5 times then every 2 rows 3 times. 48 (52, 56) sts.
At 12¼ (13¾, 15¼)" (31 [35, 39] cm), bind off the center 10 (12, 14) sts and work each side separately. Bind off along the neckline every 2 rows: 3 sts 1 time, 1 st 1 time then bind off 1 st after 4 rows.
Continue on the 11 (12, 13) sts. At 13¾ (15¼, 17¼)" (35 [39, 44] cm) work a 1 st buttonhole in the center. Bind off at 14¼ (15¾, 17¼)" (36 [40, 44] cm).

Back

Work as for the front omitting the neckline shaping.
At 13¾ (15¼, 17)" (35 [39, 43] cm), bind off the center 26 (28, 30) sts. Work each side separately for 1" (3 cm) then bind off.

Pockets x 2

Cast on 20 sts on larger needles. Work 2¼" (5.5 cm) of 2 x 2 ribbing and bind off.

Finishing

Front neckline border: Pick up and k 48 (50, 52) sts on smaller needles, along the front neckline. Work 3 rows of 2 x 2 ribbing starting with p 3 (2, 3) sts on the WS. Bind off.
Sew the sides and the inner leg seams.
Sew the pockets on the front.
Sew a button on the back for each strap.

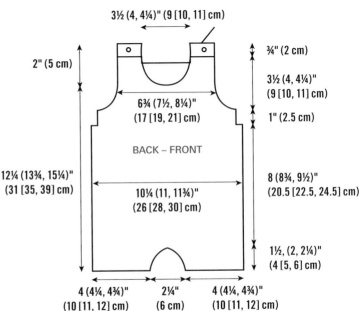

3½ (4, 4¼)" (9 [10, 11] cm)

¾" (2 cm)

2" (5 cm)

3½ (4, 4¼)" (9 [10, 11] cm)

6¾ (7½, 8¼)" (17 [19, 21] cm)

1" (2.5 cm)

BACK – FRONT

12¼ (13¾, 15¼)" (31 [35, 39] cm)

8 (8¾, 9½)" (20.5 [22.5, 24.5] cm)

10¼ (11, 11¾)" (26 [28, 30] cm)

1½, (2, 2¼)" (4 [5, 6] cm)

4 (4¼, 4¾)" (10 [11, 12] cm)

2¼" (6 cm)

4 (4¼, 4¾)" (10 [11, 12] cm)

60 - *Afternoon Slippers*

No outfit is complete without the perfect pair of footwear! The Afternoon Slippers feature a comfortable and stretchy ribbed cuff for easy on and off.

SIZE

- 3 to 6 months

YARN

- Sport weight (#2 Fine)
  Phildar Phil Noé (50% cotton, 50% acrylic; 142 yds [130 m]/1.76 oz [50 g]): Ivory, 1 skein

NEEDLES

- Size US 3 (3 mm)
  Adjust needle size if necessary to obtain the correct gauge.

NOTIONS

- Two buttons; tapestry needle

GAUGE

- 22 sts and 32 rows = 4" (10 cm) in St st on larger needles

NOTES

- Booties are worked starting from the center back of the heel

Bootie

Cast on 11 sts on smaller needles. Work in St st.
At ¾" (2 cm) cast on 4 st at the right for the half sole. 15 sts.
At 2¼" (6 cm) cast on 4 st at the left for the half top of the foot. 19 sts.
At 4" (10 cm) bind off 4 sts at each side. 11 sts. For the toe work for 1½" (4 cm) then add 4 sts to each side. At 7¾" (20 cm) bind off the 4 sts at the left and at 8¾" (22 cm) bind off 4 sts at the right. At 9½" (24 cm) bind off the rest.

Finishing

To form the welt at the edge of the sole: fold the knitting WS together along the 2nd of the first 11 sts for the entire length. Seam 1½ sts in from the fold line (3 sts total in the welt) Sew the top of the foot along the bound off edges on each half. Seam the sole joining A and B.
Border: Pick up and k 38 sts along the foot opening. Work 3 rows of 2 x 2 ribbing. Bind off and seam the heel joining T to T. Seam the edges of the sole. Sew a button on the top of each bootie.

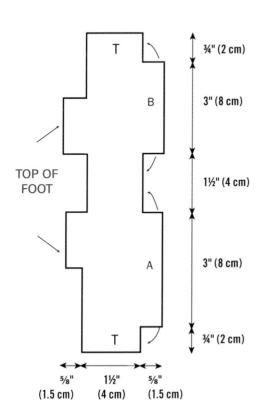

TOP OF FOOT

T

B — 3" (8 cm)

¾" (2 cm)

1½" (4 cm)

A — 3" (8 cm)

T — ¾" (2 cm)

⅝" (1.5 cm)   1½" (4 cm)   ⅝" (1.5 cm)

61 – Scholar Cardigan

Yarn: DK weight (#3 Light)

Sizes: 1 to 3 months (6 months, 12 months)

Needles: Size US 1 (2.5 mm) and Size US 2 (3 mm)

62 – Scholar's Apprentice

Yarn: Sport weight (#2 Fine) and DK weight (#3 Light)

Size: About 8" (20 cm) tall

Needles: Size US 2 (3 mm) and Size US 6 (4 mm)

61 - *Scholar Cardigan*

It's never too early to start learning! This classic professor sweater is worked flat in pieces and then seamed. Make your little scholar a little mouse apprentice (page 140) to complete the look.

SIZES
- 1 to 3 (6 months, 12 months)

YARN
- DK weight (#3 Light)
  Phildar Phil Cotton 4 (100% cotton; 93 yds [85 m]/1.76 oz [50 g]): Elephant, 3 (4, 4) skeins

NEEDLES
- Size US 4 (3.5 mm)
  Adjust needle size if necessary to obtain the correct gauge.

NOTIONS
- Three buttons; tapestry needle

GAUGE
- 21 sts and 30 rows = 4" (10 cm) in St st

Back
Cast on 50 (54, 58) sts. Work ¾" (2 cm) of 2 x 2 ribbing starting with p 2. Continue in St st.

At 5 (6, 6¾)" (13 [15, 17] cm), shape the armholes. Bind off at each side every 2 rows: 2 sts 1 time then 3 sts 1 time. 40 (44, 48) sts.

At 8¾ (9¾, 11)" (22 [25, 28] cm), bind off the center 10 (12, 14) sts and work each side separately. Work 2 rows and then bind off 5 sts at the neckline. At 9 (10¼, 11½)" (23 [26, 29] cm), bind off 10 (11, 12) shoulder sts.

Right Front
Cast on 25 (27, 29) sts. Work ¾" (2 cm) of 2 x 2 ribbing starting with k 3. Continue in St st.

At 5 (6, 6¾)" (13 [15, 17] cm), shape the neckline by dec 1 st at the right edge every 2 rows 10 (11, 12) times and **AT THE SAME TIME,** shape the armhole at the left edge as for the back.

At 9 (10¼, 11½)" (23 [26, 29] cm), bind off 10 (11, 12) shoulder sts.

Left Front

Work the same, reversing the shaping.

Sleeves x 2

Cast on 30 (34, 34) sts. Work ¾" (2 cm) of 2 x 2 ribbing then change to St st. Evenly inc 2 (0, 2) sts on the 1st row then inc 1 st at each side as follows:

1 to 3 months: Every 4 rows 6 times. 44 sts.

6 months: Every 5 rows 7 times. 48 sts.

12 months: every 5 rows 8 times. 52 sts.

At 4¼ (5½, 6¼)" (11 [14, 16] cm), bind off at each side every 2 rows: 1 st 3 times, then 2 sts 1 time. Bind off the rest.

Pockets x 2

Cast on 16 sts. Work 2" (5 cm) in St st, ¾" (2 cm) of 2 x 2 ribbing starting and ending with k3. Bind off.

Finishing

Sew the shoulders.

Border: Pick up and k 31 (33, 35) sts along the straight edge of each front, 20 (22, 24) sts along the front neckline slope and 22 (24, 26) sts along the back neckline. Work 6 rows of 2 x 2 ribbing making 3, 1 st buttonholes on row 3, the first 3 sts in from one edge and the others spaced every 11 (12, 14) sts. Bind off.

Seam sleeves to the armhole. Seam the sleeves and sides. Sew the pockets on the fronts. Sew on buttons.

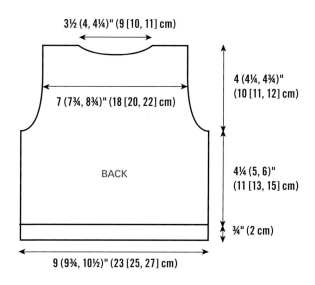

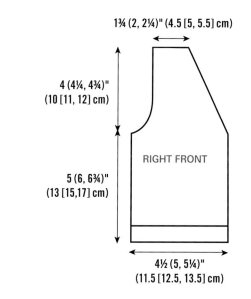

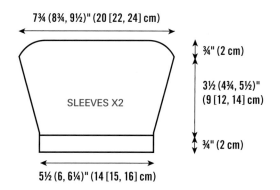

62 - *Scholar's Apprentice*

Sometimes little learners need a helping hand! This knitted scholarly mouse makes the perfect companion.

SIZE
- About 7¾" (20 cm) tall

YARN
- Sport weight (#2 Fine)
  Phildar Lambswool (51% wool, 49% acrylic; 147 yds [134 m]/1.76 oz [50 g]): Flanelle (MC), 1 skein
  Phildar Phil Cotton 3 (100% cotton; 132 yds [121 m]/1.76 oz [50 g]): Mercure (CC1), 1 skein
- DK weight (#3 Light)
  Phildar Phil Cotton 4 (100% cotton; 93 yds [85 m]/1.76 oz [50 g]): Elephant (CC2), 1 skein

NEEDLES
- Size US 2 (3 mm) and Size US 4 (3.5 mm)
  Adjust needle size if necessary to obtain the correct gauge.

NOTIONS
- Synthetic cotton; several strands of black yarn; tapestry needle

GAUGE
- 27 sts and 35 rows = 4" (10 cm) in St st using smaller needles and MC

Body
Cast on 13 sts in MC on smaller needles. Work in St st. At 2¼" (5.5 cm) put on hold. Work the left leg the same then cast on 4 st for the crotch and work the left leg sts. 30 sts.
At 4" (10.5 cm) cast on 11 st at each side for the arms. 52 sts.
At 5" (12.5 cm) you are at the top of the body. Now work top down, reversing the directions.

Head x 2
Cast on 7 sts in MC on smaller needles. Work in St st following the chart as outlined shaping with inc and dec.

Ears
Outer Ears x 2: Cast on 10 sts in MC on smaller needles. Work in St st following the chart for MC.
Inner Ears x 2: Cast on 11 sts in CC1 on smaller needles. Work in St st following the chart for CC1.

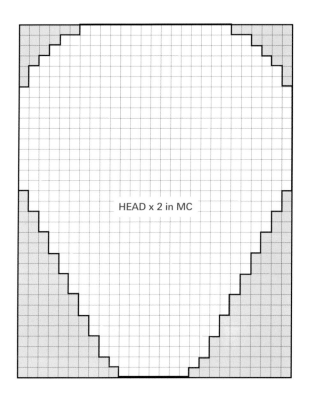

HEAD x 2 in MC

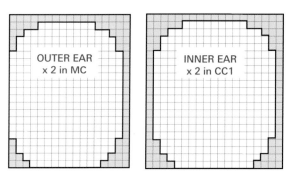

OUTER EAR
x 2 in MC

INNER EAR
x 2 in CC1

Finishing

Fold the body and seam the top of the arms, the leg inseam, and the sides leaving an opening. Place a MC thread through the ends of the arms and feet and pull tightly and attach the end firmly. Fill with stuffing and seam closed.

Sew the 2 halves of the head leaving an opening. Fill with stuffing and seam closed. Sew the CC1 ear on the MC ear then sew the sleeves on each side of the head.

Place the head to the top of the body with a 1½" (4 cm) overlap. Sew the back of the head to the top of the body and the bottom of the muzzle to the front of the body. Embroider the eyes, whiskers, and nose with straight sts in black (see photo).

Overalls

Cast on 27 sts in CC2 on larger needles. P 1 row on the RS. Work to 1½" (4 cm) then put on hold. Work the 2nd leg the same then cast on 2 sts for the crotch and work the other leg. 60 sts.

At 4¼" (11 cm) bind off 19 sts (half back and bottom of the arms). K 5 sts for the strap, bind off 12 st along the middle front and work 5 sts for the other strap and bind off the remaining 19 sts (bottom of the arm and half back).

Make the 5 st strap 4¼" (11 cm) and bind off.

Pocket

Cast on 18 sts in CC1 on smaller needles. P 1 row on the RS then change to St st. Dec 1 st at each side on rows 12, 14, and 15. Bind off.

Finishing

Borders: Pick up and k 44 sts in MC on larger needles along the outer edge of a strap and the 19 bound off sts. P 1 row on the RS then bind off. Repeat on other side. Pick up and k 64 sts along the inside border of the straps and the middle front and work the same.

Fold the overalls and seam the back and then each leg. Sew the pocket to the middle front. Put on the mouse and cross the straps in the back and attach to the center back.

63 - Artist's Tunic

Reminiscent of a panter's smock, the Artist's Tunic is an ideal knit for any future Rembrandt, Monet, or O'Keeffe. For more subtle side closures, omit the front buttonholes and sew garment snaps along the interior sides.

SIZES

- 1 to 3 (6 months, 12 months)

YARN

- Sport weight (#2 Fine)
  Phildar Lambswool (51% wool, 49% acrylic; 147 yds [134 m]/1.76 oz [50 g]): Flanelle, 2 (2, 3) skeins

NEEDLES

- Size US 1 (2.5 mm) and Size US 2 (3 mm)
  Adjust needle size if necessary to obtain the correct gauge.

NOTIONS

- Six buttons; tapestry needle

GAUGE

- 26 sts and 36 rows = 4" (10 cm) in St st on larger needles

Back

Cast on 67 (73, 79) sts on larger needles. Work 4 rows in garter st then change to St st.
At 5½ (6¼, 7)" (14 [16, 18] cm), shape the armholes. Bind off at each side every 2 rows: 3 sts 1 time, 2 sts 2 times, and 1 st 3 times. 47 (53, 59) sts. At 9½ (10½, 11¾)" (24 [27, 30] cm), bind off the center 17 (19, 23) sts and work each side separately. Work 2 rows then bind off 5 sts at the neckline. At 9¾ (11, 12¼)" (25 [28, 31] cm) bind off the remaining 10 (12, 13) shoulder sts.

Front

Work as for the back but make 3, 1 st buttonholes at each side, the first on row 6, the second on row 24 (27, 30), and the third on row 42 (47, 53).
At 6¼ (7, 7¾)" (16 [18, 20] cm), form the V-neck by binding off the center st and work each side separately, dec 1 st along the neckline every 2 rows: 13 (14, 16) times.
At 9¾ (11, 12¼)" (25 [28, 31] cm), bind off all 10 (12, 13) shoulder sts.

Pocket

Cast on 37 sts on larger needles. Work 3" (8 cm) in St st then 3 rows in garter st and bind off.

Finishing

Sew the left shoulder.
Neckline Border: With smaller needles, pick up and k 30 (32, 34) sts along the back neckline, 25 (28, 31) sts along one side of the V-neck, 1 in the center of the V, 25 (28, 31) sts along the other V. Work 3 rows in garter st and bind off.
Sides and Armholes Border: With smaller needles pick up and k 36 (42, 48) sts along back or front side edge, 64 (70, 76) sts along the armhole and 36 (42, 48) sts on the front or back edge. Work the border the same as for the neckline and bind off. Sew the pocket to the middle front.
Sew on buttons.

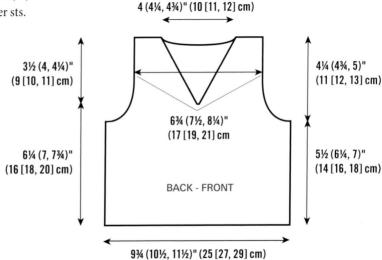

4 (4¼, 4¾)" (10 [11, 12] cm)

3½ (4, 4¼)" (9 [10, 11] cm)

4¼ (4¾, 5)" (11 [12, 13] cm)

6¾ (7½, 8¼)" (17 [19, 21] cm

6¼ (7, 7¾)" (16 [18, 20] cm)

5½ (6¼, 7)" (14 [16, 18] cm)

BACK - FRONT

9¾ (10½, 11½)" (25 [27, 29] cm)

Boutique Baby

64 – Lace Edge Bonnet

Yarn: Sport weight (#2 Fine)
Sizes: 1 to 3 months (6 to 12 months)
Needles: Size US 2 (3 mm) and Size US 4 (3.5 mm)

65 – Eyelet Wrap Front Cardigan

Yarn: Sport weight (#2 Fine)
Sizes: 3 months (6 months, 12 months)
Needles: Size US 4 (3.5 mm)

64 - Lace Edge Bonnet

SIZES
- 1 to 3 months (6 to 12 months)

YARN
- Sport weight (#2 Fine)
  Phildar Phil Noé (50% cotton, 50% acrylic; 142 yds [130 m]/1.76 oz [50 g]): Œillet, 1 skein

NEEDLES
- Size US 3 (3 mm) and Size US 4 (3.5 mm)
  Adjust needle size if necessary to obtain the correct gauge.

NOTIONS
- Cable needle; Size US B1 (2.5 mm) crochet hook; tapestry needle

GAUGE
- 22 sts and 32 rows = 4" (10 cm) in St st on larger needles

SPECIAL STITCHES
- **Eyelets:** *k 2 tog, k 1, YO *
- **Crochet border:** Along the edge of the knitting, in the same st work: *sc, half dc, dc, 1 half dc and sc. Skip 2 sts*. Repeat from * to *

Bonnet
Cast on 82 (86) sts on smaller needles. Work as follows: k 2 rows, p 1 row, 1 eyelet row, k 2 rows. Change to larger needles and continue in St st.
At 2¼ (3)" (6 [8] cm), shape the crown as follows: 1 edge stitch, * sl 2 sts to cable needle and hold in front then k together the first st on the cable needle with the first st on the left needle, k 16 (17) sts * 4 times, 1 edge stitch.
Repeat these dec on top of each other every 2 rows until there are 10 (14) sts.

Finishing
Pass the yarn through the sts and pull tightly. Seam the bonnet. Crochet a border around the brim.

65 - Eyelet Wrap Front Cardigan

SIZES
- 3 months (6 months, 12 months)

YARN
- Sport weight (#2 Fine)
  Phildar Phil Noé (50% cotton, 50% acrylic; 142 yds [130 m]/1.76 oz [50 g]): Œillet, 2 (3, 4) skeins

NEEDLES
- Size US 4 (3.5 mm)
  Adjust needle size if necessary to obtain the correct gauge.

NOTIONS
- Cable needle; size US B-1 (2.25 mm) crochet hook; two garment snaps; tapestry needle

GAUGE
- 22 sts and 32 rows = 4" (10 cm) in St st

SPECIAL STITCHES
- **Eyelets:** *k 2 tog, k 1, YO *
- **Lace Pattern**
  Row 1: k
  Row 2 and every even row: p
  Row 3: *k4, YO, k2 tog *
  Row 5 and 7: k
  Row 9: *k1, YO, k2 tog, k3
  Row 11: k
  Row 13 begin pattern again on row 1
- **Right dec:** sl 1, k 1, pass slipped st over
- **Crochet border:** along the edge of the knitting, in the same st work: *sc, half dc, dc, 1 half dc and sc. Skip 2 sts*repeat *to*

Back
Cast on 53 (57, 61) sts. K 2 rows, p 1 row, 1 eyelet row, p 2 rows then change to St st.
At 5 (6, 6¾)" (13 [15, 17] cm) bind off 1 at each edge 2 sts 1 time, then 1 st 4 times. 41 (45, 49) sts
At 8¾ (9¾, 11)" (22 [25, 28] cm), bind of the center 11 (13, 15) sts and work each side separately. Work 2 rows then bind off 5 sts at the neckline. At 9 (10¼, 11½)" (23 [26, 29] cm), bind off 10 (11, 12) shoulder sts.

Finishing

Pick up and k 17 (20, 23) sts along the straight edge of each front, k 1 row on the WS and bind off.

Sew the shoulders. Seam sleeves to the armhole. Seam the sleeves and sides. Crochet a border around the cuffs, along the front slopes and back neckline. Sew snaps between the fronts to keep them crossed.

Chain or make a small cord and make a bow and sew to the right front as shown.

Right Front

Cast on 45(49, 53) sts. Work as for the back but start the 12 row lace pattern (*see Special Stitches*) on the 2nd row of St st above the ribbing.

At 3 (3½, 4)" (8 [9, 10] cm), dec 1 st (k2tog), 1 st in from the right edge: every row 11 times, then every 2 rows 18 (21, 24) times.

AT THE SAME TIME, at 5 (6, 6¾)" (13 [15, 17] cm) bind off along the left armhole as for the back.

At 9 (10¼, 11½)" (23 [26, 29] cm) bind off 10 (11, 12) shoulder sts.

Left Front

Work the same reversing shaping using a skp dec 1 st in from the left edge for neckline shaping.

Sleeves

Cast on 33 (35, 37) sts. Work the same border as for the back then change to St st, inc 1 st every 3 rows: 7 (8, 9) times. 47 (51, 55) sts.

At 3¾ (4½, 5¾)" (9.5 [11.5, 14.5] cm), bind off every other row at each edge: 1 st 4 times and 2 sts 1 time. Bind off the rest.

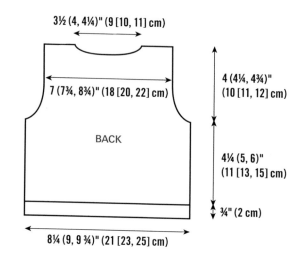

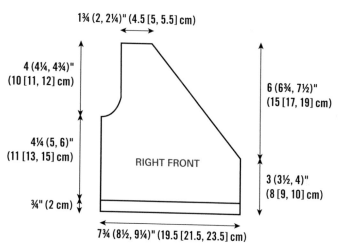

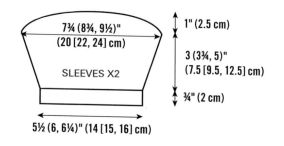

LACE PATTERN CHART

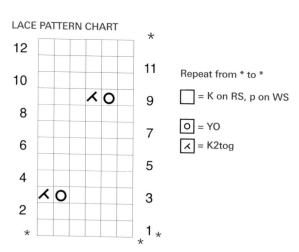

Repeat from * to *

☐ = K on RS, p on WS

◯ = YO

⋏ = K2tog

66 – Diamond Lace Blanket

Yarn: Aran weight (#4 Medium)
Size: 22¾ x 29½" (58 x 75 cm)
Needles: Size US 8 (5 mm)

68 – Simply Sweet Booties

Yarn: Fingering weight (#1 Super Fine)
Size: 3 to 6 months
Needles: Size US 1 (2.5 mm)

67 – Eyelet Lace Cardi

Yarn: Fingering weight (#1 Super Fine)
Sizes: 1 to 3 months (12 months)
Needles: Size US 1 (2.5 mm) and Size US 2 (3 mm)

69 – Daisy the Dormouse

Yarn: Fingering weight (#1 Super Fine) and Sport weight (#2 Fine)

Size: About 8" (20 cm) tall

Needles: Size US 2 (3 mm)

66 - *Diamond Lace Blanket*

Alternating squares of eyelet lace and diamond motifs make this heirloom-worthy baby blanket the ideal adornment for any nursery. Work the crocheted picot edging in a contrasting color for an added pop of interest.

SIZE
• 22¾ x 29½" (58 x 75 cm)

YARN
• Aran weight (#4 Medium)
  Phildar Adviso (60% cotton, 40% acrylic; 74 yds [68 m]/1.76 oz [50 g]): Camélia, 6 skeins

NEEDLES
• Size US 8 (5 mm)
  Adjust needle size if necessary to obtain the correct gauge.

NOTIONS
• Size US C-2 (2.75 mm) crochet hook; tapestry needle

GAUGE
• 16 sts and 24 rows = 4" (10 cm) in lace pattern

SPECIAL STITCHES
• **Lace Pattern:** Follow the chart with a 46 st and 72 row repeat between * to *
• **Single crochet:** sc
• **Chain stitch (crochet):** ch
• **Crochet Picot:** *1 sc in each of the next 3 sts, ch 3. Repeat from *working the first sc in the same st as the last sc worked

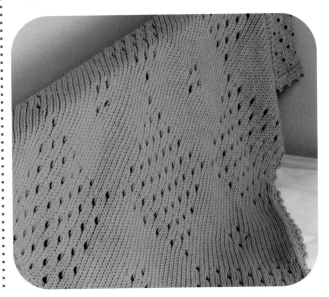

Blanket
Cast on 94 sts. Work: 1 edge st, 2 repeat of the chart, 1 edge st. Work the 72 row repeat 2 times then rows 1 to 35. Bind off.

Finishing
Crochet a row of sc then work a row of picots: *3 sc, ch 3 *

BLANKET LACE CHART

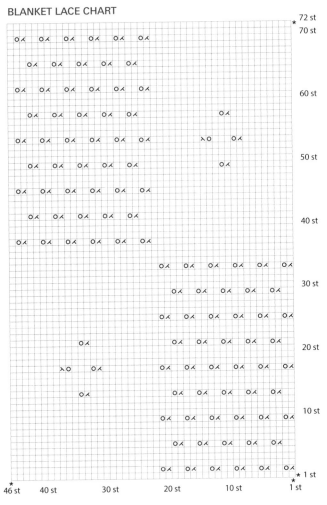

Repeat from * to *

☐	= K on WS, p on RS
⊙	= YO
⋌	= Sl 1, k1, pass slipped st over
⋋	= K2tog

67 - Eyelet Lace Cardi

Everyone will swoon over your little one in this lovely lace cardigan. Delicate eyelets adorn the sleeves and waist of this beautiful sweater, while the half-diamond lace border steals the show.

SIZES
- 1 to 3 months (12 months)

YARN
- Fingering weight (#1 Super Fine)
  Phildar Super Baby (70% acrylic, 30% wool; 117 yds [107 m]/0.88 oz [25 g]): Berlingot, 2 (3) skeins

NEEDLES
- Size US 1 (2.5 mm) and Size US 2 (3 mm)
  Adjust needle size if necessary to obtain the correct gauge.

NOTIONS
- Four buttons; size US B-1 (2.5 mm) crochet hook; tapestry needle

GAUGE
- 29 sts and 40 rows = 4" (10 cm) in St st

SPECIAL STITCHES
- **Eyelets:** *k 1, k2 tog, YO, k 1 *
- **Lace Pattern**
  Row 1: *k 1, YO, k3, skp, k2 tog, k 3, YO *
  Row 2 and every even row: p
  Row 3: *k 2, YO, k 2, skp, k2 tog, k 2, YO, k 1*
  Row 5: k 3, YO, k 1, skp, k2 tog, k 1, YO, k 2*
  Row 7: * k 4, YO, ssk, k2 tog, YO, k3*
- **Skp:** sl 1, k 1, pass slipped st over
- **Crochet Picots:** *4 sc., ch 3 *

Back
Cast on 89 (100) sts with larger needle. Work 2 rows in garter st then work the lace pattern starting at the first st on the chart (*page 152*). When the chart is worked change to St st.
At 4¾ (6¼)" (12 [16] cm), dec 22 (21) sts evenly. K a row on the WS 67 (79) sts. Work 2 rows St st, a row of eyelets, then change to St st.
At 5¾ (7¼)" (14.5 [18.5] cm), shape the armholes. Bind off every 2 rows at each edge: 3 sts 1 time, 2 sts 1 time, and 1 st 4 times. 49 (61) sts.
At 8¾ (11¼)" (22.5 [28.5] cm), bind off the center 17 (21) sts and finish each side separately. Work 2 rows then bind off 5 sts. Work straight to 9¼ (11¼)" (23.5 [29.5] cm). Bind off 11 (15) shoulder sts.

Left Front
Cast on 51 (57) sts in larger needles. Work as for the lower back.
At 4¾ (6¼)" (12 [16] cm), dec 13 st evenly. K across the WS row on the 38 (44) sts. Work 2 rows in St st, 1 row of eyelets then finish in St st.
At 5¾ (7¼)" (14.5 [18.5] cm) bind off along the right armhole as for the back. 29 (35) sts.
At 7½ (9¾)" (19 [25] cm) shape the neckline by binding off at the left side every 2 rows: 10 (12) sts 1 time, 3 sts 1 time, 2 sts 1 time, then 1 st 3 times.
At 9¼ (11¼)" (23.5 [29.5] cm) bind off 11 (15) shoulder sts.

67 - *Eyelet Lace Cardi* (continued)

Right Front

Work the same reversing shaping but making 4, 1 st buttonholes 3 sts from the front edge, the first at 3 (4¼)" (8 [11] cm), and the rest spaced every 1 (1½)" (3 [4] cm).

Sleeves

Cast on 42 (48) sts on larger needles. Work 2 rows garter st, 2 rows in St st, 1 row of eyelets then finish in St st. **AT THE SAME TIME**, inc 1 st every 5 rows at each side 6 (9) times. 54 (66) sts.

At 3½ (5½)" (9 [14] cm) bind off at each side every 2 rows: 1 st 4 times, 2 sts 1 time, then 3 sts 1 time. Bind off the remaining sts.

Finishing

Front Borders: Pick up and k 49 (67) sts on smaller needles along the front edge. K 1 row on the WS and then bind off. Repeat on the other edge.

Sew the shoulders.

Neckline Border: Pick up and k 82 (100) sts on smaller needles around the neckline. K 1 row on the WS then bind off.

Seam sleeves in the armhole. Seam the sleeves and sides. Sew on buttons.

Crochet picots around the neckline, the cuffs and the hem of the cardigan.

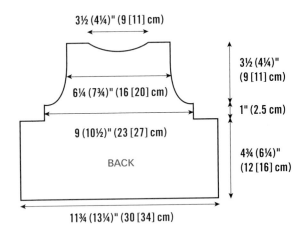

3½ (4¼)" (9 [11] cm)

3½ (4¼)" (9 [11] cm)

1" (2.5 cm)

6¼ (7¾)" (16 [20] cm)

9 (10½)" (23 [27] cm)

BACK

4¾ (6¼)" (12 [16] cm)

11¾ (13¼)" (30 [34] cm)

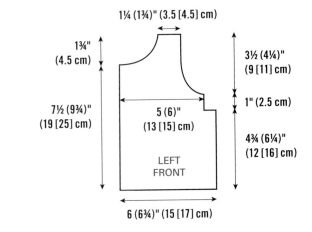

1¼ (1¾)" (3.5 [4.5] cm)

1¾" (4.5 cm)

3½ (4¼)" (9 [11] cm)

1" (2.5 cm)

7½ (9¾)" (19 [25] cm)

5 (6)" (13 [15] cm)

4¾ (6¼)" (12 [16] cm)

LEFT FRONT

6 (6¾)" (15 [17] cm)

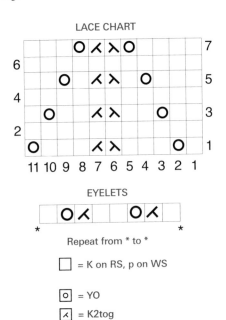

LACE CHART

7

6

5

4

3

2

1

11 10 9 8 7 6 5 4 3 2 1

EYELETS

★   ★

Repeat from * to *

☐ = K on RS, p on WS

Ⓞ = YO

☑ = K2tog

☒ = Skp

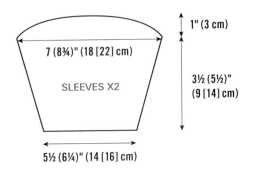

1" (3 cm)

7 (8¾)" (18 [22] cm)

SLEEVES X2

3½ (5½)" (9 [14] cm)

5½ (6¼)" (14 [16] cm)

68 - *Simply Sweet Booties*

You can never have enough booties for your baby! This is the perfect pattern for using up leftover yarn from other projects!

SIZE
- 3 to 6 months

YARN
- Fingering weight (#1 Super Fine)
  Phildar Super Baby (70% acrylic, 30% wool; 117 yds [107 m]/0.88 oz [25 g]): Berlingot, 1 skein

NEEDLES
- Size US 2 (3 mm)
  Adjust needle size if necessary to obtain the correct gauge.

NOTIONS
- Size US B-1 (2.5 mm) crochet hook; tapestry needle

GAUGE
- 29 sts and 40 rows = 4" (10 cm) in St st

NOTES
- Booties are worked in two pieces—the side/sole and top of foot

SPECIAL STITCHES
- **Lace Pattern:** Follow the chart for the 5 st, 5 row motif
- **Crochet Picots:** 4 sc, ch 3 *
- **Eyelets:** *k 1, k2 tog, YO, k 1 *

Sides—Sole
Cast on 12 sts (center of heel). Work in St st.
At ¾" (2 cm), cast on 5 st at the RS, Work 3" (8 cm) on the 17 sts. Bind off the first 5 sts. Work 1½" (4 cm) on the 12 sts then cast on 5 sts at the RS. Work 3" (8 cm) on the 17 sts. Bind off the first 5 sts. Work ¾" (2 cm) and bind off all 12 sts.

Top of the Foot
Cast on 13 sts and work 12 rows in St st. Work 1 row of eyelets then finish in St st. **AT THE SAME TIME,** dec 1 st at each side of row 14, 16, 17, 18, and 19. Bind off the remaining 3 sts.

Finishing
Join A to A to seam the sole. Seam the end of the foot. Sew the side to the top aligning the middle of the side and the top.
Border: Pick up and k 19 sts along the edge of the sides, 11 sts along the front, 19 st along the other side. K 1 row on WS and bind off. Crochet picots around the top edge Join B to B and seam the back of the heel.

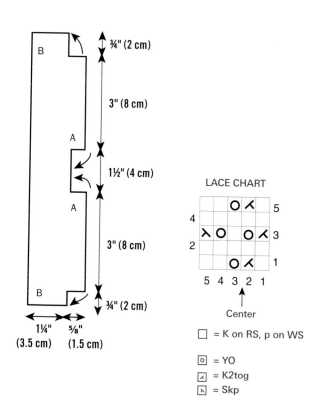

LACE CHART

= K on RS, p on WS

= YO

= K2tog

= Skp

Center

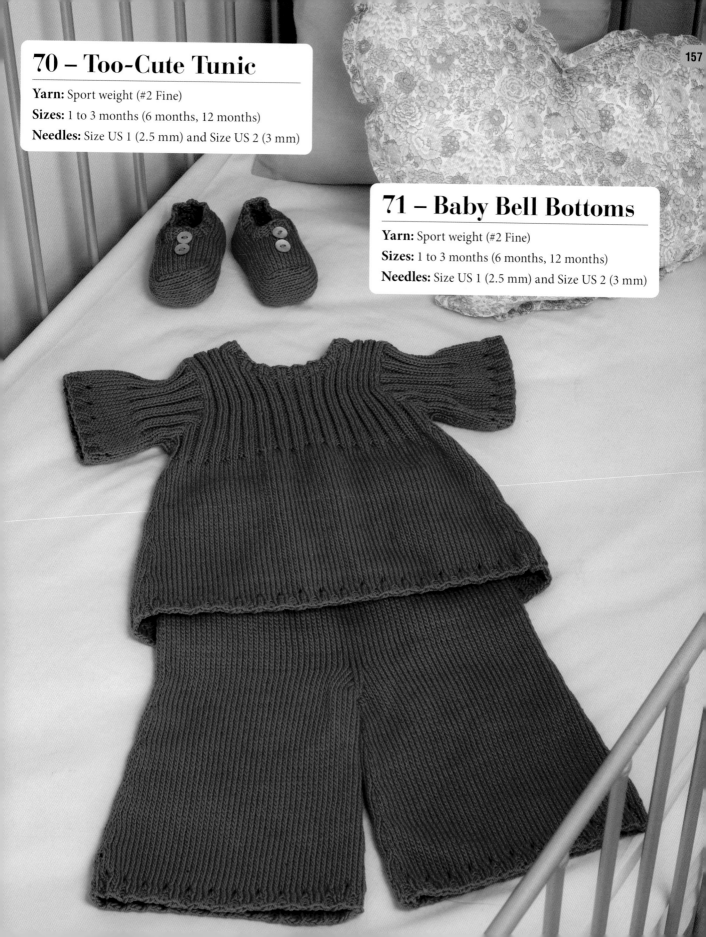

70 – Too-Cute Tunic

Yarn: Sport weight (#2 Fine)

Sizes: 1 to 3 months (6 months, 12 months)

Needles: Size US 1 (2.5 mm) and Size US 2 (3 mm)

71 – Baby Bell Bottoms

Yarn: Sport weight (#2 Fine)

Sizes: 1 to 3 months (6 months, 12 months)

Needles: Size US 1 (2.5 mm) and Size US 2 (3 mm)

70 - *Too-Cute Tunic*

Flowy and free, this tunic top has extra room for your baby to grow. Ribbing around the neckline and sleeves means fit as well as stretch. This knit is sure to have everyone saying, "Too Cute!"

SIZES
- 1 to 3 months (6 months, 12 months)

YARN
- Sport weight (#2 Fine)
  Phildar Phil Cotton 3 (100% cotton; 132 yds
  [121 m]/1.76 oz [50 g]): Clématite, 2 (3, 3) skeins

NEEDLES
- Size US 1(2.5 mm) and Size US 2 (3 mm)
  Adjust needle size if necessary to obtain the correct gauge.

NOTIONS
- Six buttons; tapestry needle

GAUGE
- 26 sts and 35 rows = 4" (10 cm) in St st on larger needles

SPECIAL STITCHES
- **Eyelets:** *k 1, k2 tog, YO, k 1 *

Front

Cast on 74 (78, 86) sts on larger needles. Work ⅜" (1 cm) of 2 x 2 ribbing starting with p 2, then change to St st. Evenly inc 0 (2, 0) sts on the first row. 74 (80, 86) sts. Work eyelets (*see Special Stitches*) on row 3. Dec 1 st at each side every 12 (14, 16) rows 4 times. 66 (72, 78) sts.
At 6½ (7¼, 8)" (16.5 [18.5, 20.5] cm), change to 2 x 2 ribbing starting with k 2 (3, 2).
At 7½ (8¼, 9)" (19 [21, 23] cm), shape the armholes by binding off at each edge every 2 rows: 2 sts 2 times, then 1 st 2 times. 54 (60, 66) sts.
At 9 (10¼, 12¼)" (23 [26, 31] cm), bind off the center 8 (10, 14) sts and work each side separately. Bind off along the neckline every 2 rows: 3 sts 1 time, 2 sts 1 time, 1 st 4 times.
At 11 (12¼, 13¼)" (28 [31, 34] cm), bind off the remaining 14 (16, 17) shoulder sts.

Half-Back

Cast on 37 (40, 43) sts on large needles. Work ⅜" (1 cm) of 2 x 2 ribbing starting with p3 (k3, p3) then change to St st working a row of eyelets as for the front. Dec as for the front at the right edge. 33 (36, 39) sts.
At 6½ (7¼, 8)" (16.5 [18.5, 20.5] cm), change to 2 x 2 ribbing shaping the armhole as for the front.
At 7½ (8¼, 9)" (19 [21, 23] cm), bind off the armhole at the left as for the front. 27 (30, 33) sts.
At 10½ (11¾, 13)" (27 [30, 33] cm), shape the neckline by binding off along the right edge every 2 rows: 8 (9, 11) sts 1 time then 5 sts 1 time.
At 11 (12¼, 13¼)" (28 [31, 34] cm), bind off the remaining 14 (16, 17) shoulder sts. Work the other half-back reversing the shaping.

Sleeves

Cast on 46 (50, 58) sts on larger needles. Work ⅜" (1 cm) of 2 x 2 ribbing. Change to St st. Inc 0 (2, 0) sts evenly on row 1. 46 (52, 58) sts working eyelets on row 3. At 2¼ (3, 3¾)" (5.5 [7.5, 9.5] cm) change to 2 x 2 ribbing, starting and ending with k 2 (3, 2).
At 3 (4, 4¾)" (8 [10, 12] cm) bind off at each edge every 2 rows: 1 st 2 times and 2 sts 2 times. Bind off the rest.

Finishing

Sew the shoulders.

Neckline Border: Pick up and k 72 (76, 84) sts on smaller needles, along the neckline. Work 3 rows of 2 x 2 ribbing starting and ending with p3. Bind off.

Button Bands: Pick up and k 68 (76, 84) sts on smaller needles at the edge of a half-back. Work as for the neckline border. On the other border make 6, 1 st buttonholes on row 1. Place the first 3 sts below the neckline or 9 (7, 10) sts from the bottom and the rest 10 (12, 13) sts apart. Seam sleeves to the armhole. Seam the sleeves and sides. Sew on buttons.

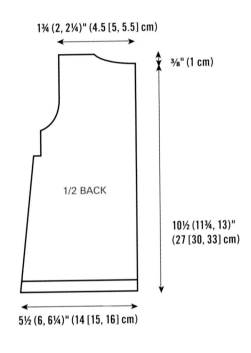

1¾ (2, 2¼)" (4.5 [5, 5.5] cm)

⅜" (1 cm)

1/2 BACK

10½ (11¾, 13)" (27 [30, 33] cm)

5½ (6, 6¼)" (14 [15, 16] cm)

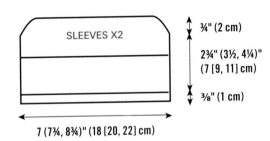

SLEEVES X2

¾" (2 cm)

2¾ (3½, 4¼)" (7 [9, 11] cm)

⅜" (1 cm)

7 (7¾, 8¾)" (18 [20, 22] cm)

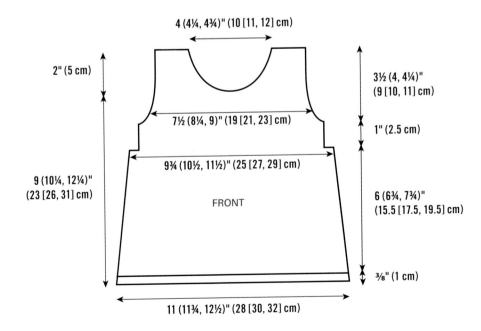

4 (4¼, 4¾)" (10 [11, 12] cm)

2" (5 cm)

3½ (4, 4¼)" (9 [10, 11] cm)

7½ (8¼, 9)" (19 [21, 23] cm)

1" (2.5 cm)

9¾ (10½, 11½)" (25 [27, 29] cm)

9 (10¼, 12¼)" (23 [26, 31] cm)

FRONT

6 (6¾, 7¾)" (15.5 [17.5, 19.5] cm)

⅜" (1 cm)

11 (11¾, 12½)" (28 [30, 32] cm)

71 - *Baby Bell Bottoms*

Not your aunt's bell bottoms! Vintage style with a modern update, these bell-bottomed baby pants are a fun addition to any warm day outfit.

SIZES

- 1 to 3 months (6 months, 12 months)

YARN

- Sport weight (#2 Fine)
  Phildar Phil Cotton 3 (100% cotton; 132 yds [121 m]/1.76 oz [50 g]): Clématite, 2 (3, 3) skeins

NEEDLES

- Size US 1 (2.5 mm) and Size US 2 (3 mm)
  Adjust needle size if necessary to obtain the correct gauge.

NOTIONS

- Elastic thread: tapestry needle

GAUGE

- 28 sts and 34 rows = 4" (10 cm) in St st on larger needles

SPECIAL STITCHES

- **Eyelets:** *k 1, k2tog, YO, k 1 *

Back

Cast on 54 (57, 60) sts on smaller needles. Work ⅜" (1 cm) in 2 x 2 ribbing then change to St st using larger needles forming eyelets on row 3. Dec 1 st at each side every: 8 (9, 10) rows 7 times. At 6¼ (7, 7¾)" (16 [18, 20] cm) put the 40 (43, 46) sts on hold. Work the right leg the same then take up the left leg sts and work 80 (86, 92) sts. To shape the crotch, dec 1 st at either side of the center 2 sts every row 3 times then every 2 rows 3 times. 68 (74, 80) sts. At 12¼ (13¼, 14½)" (31 [34, 37] cm), change to smaller needles and work 1" (3 cm) 1 x 1 ribbing. Bind off.

Front

Work as for the back.

Finishing

Sew the sides.
Seam the inseams.
Thread several rows of elastic thread under the waist ribbing.

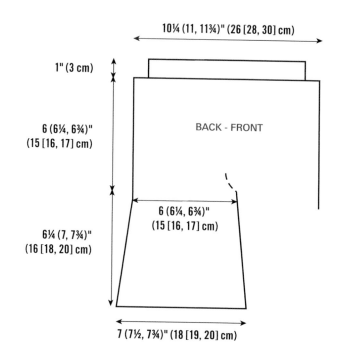

10¼ (11, 11¾)" (26 [28, 30] cm)

1" (3 cm)

6 (6¼, 6¾)"
(15 [16, 17] cm)

BACK - FRONT

6 (6¼, 6¾)"
(15 [16, 17] cm)

6¼ (7, 7¾)"
(16 [18, 20] cm)

7 (7½, 7¾)" (18 [19, 20] cm)

72 – Buttoned Baby Slippers

Yarn: Sport weight (#2 Fine)

Size: 3 to 6 months

Needles: Size US 1 (2.5 mm) and Size US 2 (3 mm)

73 – Pretty Pocket Dress

Yarn: DK weight (#3 Light)

Sizes: 1 to 3 months (6 months, 12 months)

Needles: Size US 4 (3.5 mm) and Size US 6 (4 mm)

72 - *Buttoned Baby Slippers*

Looking for an easy knitted baby slipper? This pattern is quick, easy, and sure to please even the pickiest tot! Change things up by swapping out the buttons for a cute little bow instead!

SIZE
- 3 to 6 months

YARN
- Sport weight (#2 Fine)
  Phildar Phil Cotton 3 (100% cotton; 132 yds [121 m]/1.76 oz [50 g]): Clématite, 1 skein

NEEDLES
- Size US 1(2.5 mm) and Size US 2 (3 mm)
  Adjust needle size if necessary to obtain the correct gauge.

NOTIONS
- Four buttons; tapestry needle

GAUGE
- 28 sts and 34 rows = 4" (10 cm) in St st on larger needles

NOTES
- Booties are worked in one piece starting with the back of the heel

Booties
Cast on 11 sts on larger needle. Work in St st. At ¾" (2 cm), cast on 5 sts at the right (half-sole). 16 sts
At 2¼" (6 cm), cast on 5 st at the left (half foot). 21 sts.
At 4" (10 cm), bind off 5 st at each side.
For the toe end, continue on the 11 sts for 1½" (4 cm) then cast on 5 sts at each edge.
At 7¾" (20 cm), bind off 5 st at the left, and at 8¾" (22 cm) bind off 5 st on the right. At 9½" (24 cm) bind off the remaining 11 sts.

Finishing
Fold the slipper joining A and B. Sew the sole seam.
Border: Pick up and k 38 sts on larger needles around the top opening. Work 3 rows of 2 x 2 ribbing. Bind off.
Join T to T and sew the heel and edges of the sole. Sew 2 buttons to the top of each slipper.

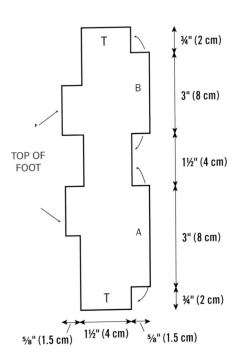

73 - *Pretty Pocket Dress*

SIZES
- 1 to 3 months (6 months, 12 months)

YARN
- DK weight (#3 Light)
  Phildar Phil Cotton 4 (100% cotton; 93 yds
  [85 m]/1.76 oz [50 g]): Bengale, 3 (4, 5) skeins

NEEDLES
- Size US 4 (3.5 mm) and Size US 6 (4 mm)
  *Adjust needle size if necessary to obtain the
  correct gauge.*

NOTIONS
- Two buttons; tapestry needle

GAUGE
- 21 sts and 30 rows = 4" (10 cm) in St st on
  larger needles

Back

Cast on 66 (70, 74) sts on larger needles. Work ⅜" (1 cm) of 2 x 2 ribbing. Change to St st and dec 1 st in the middle of row 1. 65 (69, 73) sts. Dec 1 st at each side every 8 (9, 10) rows 8 times. 49 (53, 57) sts.
At 8¾ (10½, 12¼)" (22 [27, 31] cm), divide the work in half to form the back opening and bind off the center st. Continue on each side separately.
At 9½ (11, 12¼)" (24 [28, 31] cm), shape the sleeve by inc every 2 rows, 1 st 2 times, then every row 1 st 1 time then 5 (7, 9) sts 1 time. 32 (36, 40) sts.
At 12½ (14½, 16)" (32 [37, 41] cm), shape the neckline by binding off every 2 rows: 7 (8, 9) sts 1 time and 3 sts 1 time.
At 13 (15, 16½)" (33 [38, 42] cm), bind off the remaining 22 (25, 28) sts.

Front

Work as for the back omitting the back opening.
At 9 (11, 12½)" (23 [28, 32] cm), put the center 13 (13, 17) sts on hold and work each side separately.
At 11½ (13½, 15¼)" (29.5 [34.5, 38.5] cm), shape the neckline by binding off every 2 rows: 2 (3, 2) sts 1 time and 1 st 2 times. At 13 (15, 16½)" (33 [38, 42] cm), bind off the remaining 22 (25, 28) sts.

Neck Placket

Cast on 1 st on smaller needles, then add the neckline sts put on hold and work as follows: * P front and back in the next st, k 2 * 4 (4, 5) times, p front and back in the last st, cast on 1 st. 20 (20, 24) sts. Work in 2 x 2 ribbing starting and ending with k3 on the RS.
At 2¼" (6 cm), bind off the center 10 (10, 14) sts and work each side separately. Bind off along the neckline every 2 rows: 3 sts 1 time and 2 sts 1 time.

Pockets x 2

Cast on 20 sts on smaller needles. Work 2¼" (6 cm) of 2 x 2 ribbing starting and ending with k3. Bind off.

Finishing

Sew the shoulder and top of sleeves seam.
Neckline Border: Pick up and k 64 (68, 72) sts on smaller needles around the neckline. Work 3 rows of 2 x 2 ribbing starting and ending with p3. Bind off.
Button Bands: Pick up and k 24 sts on smaller needles, starting at the end of the back opening. Work 3 rows of 2 x 2 ribbing starting and ending with k3. Bind off. Repeat on the other side working 2, 1 st buttonholes, the first 3 sts from the neckband and the 2nd, 10 sts from the first.
Overlap and sew the 2 borders to the mid back.
Sleeve Borders: Pick up and k 34 (38, 42) sts on larger needles at the end of each sleeve. Work 3 rows of 2 x 2 ribbing starting and ending with k 2. Bind off.
Sew the sides and bottom of the sleeves. Seam the pockets to the front. Sew on buttons.

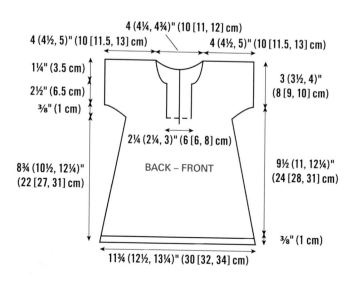

4 (4¼, 4¾)" (10 [11, 12] cm)
4 (4½, 5)" (10 [11.5, 13] cm)
4 (4½, 5)" (10 [11.5, 13] cm)
1¼" (3.5 cm)
2½" (6.5 cm)
⅜" (1 cm)
3 (3½, 4)" (8 [9, 10] cm)
2¼ (2¼, 3)" (6 [6, 8] cm)
8¾ (10½, 12¼)" (22 [27, 31] cm)
BACK – FRONT
9½ (11, 12¼)" (24 [28, 31] cm)
⅜" (1 cm)
11¾ (12½, 13¼)" (30 [32, 34] cm)

Bold and Beautiful Knits

74 – Traveler Coat

Yarn: Bulky weight (#5 Bulky)
Sizes: 3 months (6 months, 12 months)
Needles: Size US 7 (4.5 mm) and Size US 8 (5 mm)

75 – Panda Pal

Yarn: Sport weight (#2 Fine) and Bulky weight (#5 Bulky)
Size: About 8" (20 cm) tall
Needles: Size US 2 (3 mm) and Size US 4 (3.5 mm)

76 – Sightseer Pullover

Yarn: Sport weight (#2 Fine)
Sizes: 3 months (6 months, 12 months)
Needles: Size US 1 (2.5 mm) and Size US 2 (3 mm)

74 - *Traveler Coat*

What journies your little one could have while wearing this coat! Add the decorative embroidered dotted lines after you finish knitting, or leave it a solid color for a more subdued wardrobe staple.

SIZES
- 3 months (6 months, 12 months)

YARN
- Bulky weight (#5 Bulky)
  Phildar Partner 6 (50% polyamide, 25% wool, 25% acrylic; 71 yds [65 m]/1.76 oz [50 g]): Noir (MC), 5 (6, 7) skeins; Blanc (CC), 1 skein

NEEDLES
- Size US 8 (5 mm)
  Adjust needle size if necessary to obtain the correct gauge.

NOTIONS
- Three white buttons; tapestry needle

GAUGE
- 17 sts and 23 rows = 4" (10 cm) in St st

Back
Cast on 46 (50, 54) sts in MC. Work ¾" (2 cm) of 1 x 1 ribbing then change to St st.
At 6 (6¾, 7½)" (15 [17, 19] cm), shape the armhole by binding off at each edge, every 2 rows: 2 sts 2 times and 1 st 2 times. 38 (42, 46) sts. At 9¾ (11, 12¼)" (25 [28, 31] cm), bind off the center 6 (8, 10) sts and work each side separately. Work 2 rows and bind off 4 sts at the neckline. At 10¼ (11½, 12½)" (26 [29, 32] cm), bind off the remaining 12 (13, 14) shoulder sts.

Right Front
Cast on 24 (26, 28) sts in MC. Work as for the back. At 6 (6¾, 7½)" (15 [17, 19] cm), shape the armhole at the left edge as for the back. 20 (22, 24) sts. At 8¾ (9¾, 11)" (22 [25, 28] cm), shape the neckline by binding off at the right edge every 2 rows: 3 (4, 5) sts 1 time, 3 sts 1 time and 1 st 2 times. At 10¼ (11½, 12½)" (26 [29, 32] cm), bind off the remaining 12 (13, 14) shoulder sts.

Left Front
Work the same, reversing the shaping.

Sleeves
Cast on 27 (29, 31) sts in MC. Work ¾" (2 cm) of 1 x 1 ribbing then change to St st. Inc 1 st at each edge every 3 rows 6 times (every 4 rows 7 times, every 4 rows 8 times). 39 (43, 47) sts. At 4 (5½, 6¼)" (10 [14, 16] cm), bind off at each side every 2 rows: 1 st 2 times and 2 sts 1 time. Bind off the remaining sts.

Hood
Cast on 23 (25, 27) sts in MC. Work in S st. Inc 1 st every 4 rows 5 times. 28 (30, 32) sts. Continue straight. At 11¼ (12¾, 14¼)" (28.5 [32.5, 36.5] cm), dec 1 st at the right edge every 4 rows 5 times. 23 (25, 27) sts. At 14½ (16, 17¾)" (37 [41, 45] cm), bind off all sts.

Pockets x 2
Cast on 14 sts in MC. Work 2¼" (6 cm) of St st then ¾" (2 cm) of 1 x 1 ribbing. Bind off.

Finishing
Hood Border: Pick up and k 67 (73, 79) sts in MC, along the straight edge of the hood. Work 3 rows of 1 x 1 ribbing and bind off.
Button Bands: Pick up and k 39 (45, 51) sts in MC, along a front edge. Work 3 rows of 1 x 1 ribbing and bind off. Work the buttonhole band on the other side, making 3, 1 st buttonholes on the first row with the first, 3 st from the neck border and the rest spaced 9 (11, 13) sts apart.
Sew the shoulders. Seam sleeves to the armhole. Seam the sleeves and sides. Sew the back of the hood then sew to the neck with the middle of the button band overlapping the other.
Sew the pockets to the middle of the fronts, 1" (3 cm) above the hem.
Embroider lines on the back and fronts with CC. A vertical line on either side of the neckline including on the pockets, a horizontal line at the level of the armhole, another just above the lower ribbing and the third 1 (1½, 2)" (3 [4, 5] cm) above the lower. Embroider a horizontal line in the middle of the hood, and another 2 (2¼, 2¾)" (5 [6, 7] cm) lower. Embroider a horizontal line just above the sleeve ribbing then another along the top of the sleeve at right angles to the top one on the body.

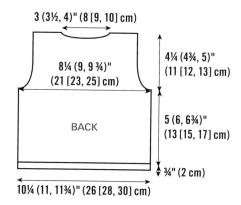

3 (3½, 4)" (8 [9, 10] cm)

8¼ (9, 9 ¾)"
(21 [23, 25] cm)

4¼ (4¾, 5)"
(11 [12, 13] cm)

BACK

5 (6, 6¾)"
(13 [15, 17] cm)

¾" (2 cm)

10¼ (11, 11¾)" (26 [28, 30] cm)

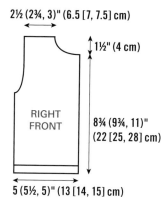

2½ (2¾, 3)" (6.5 [7, 7.5] cm)

1½" (4 cm)

RIGHT
FRONT

8¾ (9¾, 11)"
(22 [25, 28] cm)

5 (5½, 5)" (13 [14, 15] cm)

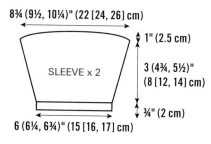

8¾ (9½, 10¼)" (22 [24, 26] cm)

1" (2.5 cm)

SLEEVE x 2

3 (4¾, 5½)"
(8 [12, 14] cm)

¾" (2 cm)

6 (6¼, 6¾)" (15 [16, 17] cm)

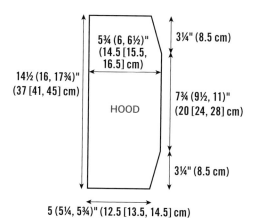

5¾ (6, 6½)"
(14.5 [15.5, 16.5] cm)

3¼" (8.5 cm)

14½ (16, 17¾)"
(37 [41, 45] cm)

HOOD

7¾ (9½, 11)"
(20 [24, 28] cm)

3¼" (8.5 cm)

5 (5¼, 5¾)" (12.5 [13.5, 14.5] cm)

75 - Panda Pal

Every great adventure is better with a companion! This cuddly knitted friend is made with patches of fuzzy faux-fur yarn for extra snuggliness and is ready to hit the road with your baby.

SIZE
• About 8" (20 cm) tall

YARN
• Sport weight (#2 Fine)
Phildar Partner 3.5 (50% polyamide, 25% wool, 25% acrylic; 71 yds [65 m]/1.76 oz [50 g]): White (C1), 1 skein
• Bulky weight (#5 Bulky)
Phildar Phil Douce (90% acrylic, 10% polyamide; 94 yds [86 m]/1.76 oz [50 g]): Noir (C2), 1 skein

NEEDLES
• Size US 2 (3 mm) and Size US 4 (3.5 mm)
Adjust needle size if necessary to obtain the correct gauge.

NOTIONS
• Synthetic stuffing; tapestry needle

GAUGE
• 25 sts and 34 rows = 4" (10 cm) in St st in C1 using smaller needles

77 – Trail Sweater

Yarn: Fingering weight (#1 Super Fine)
Sizes: Newborn (3 months, 6 months)
Needles: Size US 1 (2.5 mm) and Size US 2 (3 mm)

78 – Simple Strappy Shoes

Yarn: Fingering weight (#1 Super Fine)
Sizes: Newborn (3 months, 6 months)
Needles: Size US 2 (3 mm)

77 - Trail Sweater

Trailing lines inspire stories yet made in this adorable staple cardigan. Customize the dotted-line colorwork motif by substituting black with your favorite colors.

SIZES
- Newborn (3 months, 6 months)

YARN
- Fingering weight (#1 Super Fine)
  Phildar Partner Baby (50% polyamide, 25% wool, 25% acrylic; 117 yds [107 m]/0.88 oz [25 g]): Blanc (MC), 2 skeins
  Phildar Super Baby (70% acrylic, 30% wool; 117 yds [107 m]/0.88 oz [25 g]): Souris (CC), 1 skein

NEEDLES
- Size US 1 (2.5 mm) and Size US 2 (3 mm)
  Adjust needle size if necessary to obtain the correct gauge.

NOTIONS
- Two black buttons; tapestry needle

GAUGE
- 31 sts and 41 rows = 4" (10 cm) in St st on larger needles

Back
Cast on 70 (76, 82) sts in MC on smaller needles. Work ⅜" (1 cm) of 1 x 1 ribbing then change to St st alternating 2 sts of CC and 2 sts of MC on row 2 only.
At 2 (2¾, 3½)" (5 [7, 9] cm), shape the armholes: bind off at each edge, every 2 rows: 3 sts 1 time, 2 sts 2 times, and 1 st 4 times.
At 5½ (6¾, 7¾)" (14 [17, 20] cm), bind off the center 12 (14, 16) sts and work each side separately. Work 2 rows then bind off 7 sts. Work straight for 6 (7, 8¼)" (15 [18, 21] cm), bind off the remaining 11 (13, 15) shoulder sts.

Right Front
Cast on 36 (39, 42) sts on smaller needles. Work as for the back.
At 2 (2¾, 3½)" (5 [7, 9] cm), bind off along the left armhole edge as for the back. 25 (28, 31) sts. At 4¼ (5½, 6¾)" (11 [14, 17] cm), shape the neckline binding off at the right edge every 2 rows: 4 (5, 6) sts 1 time, 4 sts 1 time, 2 sts 2 times, and 1 st 2 times.
At 6 (7, 8¼)" (15 [18, 21] cm), bind off the remaining11 (13, 15) shoulder sts.

Left Front
Work the same, reversing the shaping.

Sleeves
Cast on 48 (52, 56) sts in MC on smaller needles. Work ⅜" (1 cm) of 1 x 1 ribbing. Change to larger needles and work in St st alternating 2 MC and 2 CC sts on row 2 only. Inc 1 st at each side as follows: 1 st every 4 rows 8 times (every 5 rows 9 times, every 6 rows 10 times). 64 (70, 76) sts.
At 4 (5½, 6¼)" (10 [14, 16] cm), bind off every 2 rows at each side: 1 st 4 times, 2 sts 2 times and 3 sts 1 time. Bind off the rest.

Pocket
Cast on 18 sts in MC on larger needles. Work 1½" (4 cm) of St st alternating 2 MC and 2 CC sts on the next-to-last row. Change to smaller needles and work ⅜" (1 cm) of 1 x 1 ribbing and bind off.

Finishing

Sew the shoulders.

Neckline Border: Pick up and k 71 (75, 79) sts in MC in smaller needles, around the neckline. Work ⅜" (1 cm) of 1 x 1 ribbing and bind off.

Button Bands: Pick up and k 38 (53, 63) sts in MC in smaller needles along the left front edge. Work ⅜" (1 cm) of 1 x 1 ribbing and bind off. Work the buttonhole band on the other front making 2, 1 st buttonholes with the first 3 sts from the neckline, the 2nd 14 (16, 18) sts from the first.

Seam sleeves to the armhole. Seam the sleeves and sides. Sew on buttons. Sew the pocket to the top of the left front.

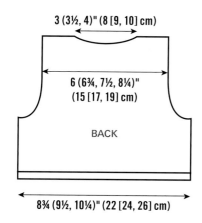

3 (3½, 4)" (8 [9, 10] cm)

6 (6¾, 7½, 8¼)"
(15 [17, 19] cm)

BACK

8¾ (9½, 10¼)" (22 [24, 26] cm)

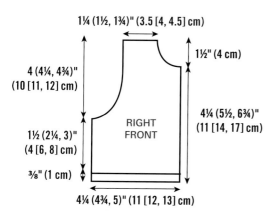

1¼ (1½, 1¾)" (3.5 [4, 4.5] cm)

1½" (4 cm)

4 (4¼, 4¾)"
(10 [11, 12] cm)

RIGHT FRONT

4¼ (5½, 6¾)"
(11 [14, 17] cm)

1½ (2¼, 3)"
(4 [6, 8] cm)

⅜" (1 cm)

4¼ (4¾, 5)" (11 [12, 13] cm)

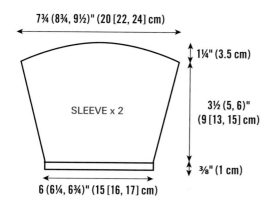

7¾ (8¾, 9½)" (20 [22, 24] cm)

1¼" (3.5 cm)

SLEEVE x 2

3½ (5, 6)"
(9 [13, 15] cm)

⅜" (1 cm)

6 (6¼, 6¾)" (15 [16, 17] cm)

78 - Simple Strappy Shoes

SIZES
- Newborn (3 months, 6 months)

YARN
- Fingering weight (#1 Super Fine) Phildar Super Baby (70% acrylic, 30% wool; 117 yds [107 m]/0.88 oz [25 g]): Souris, 1 skein

NEEDLES
- Size US 2 (3 mm)
  Adjust needle size if necessary to obtain the correct gauge.

NOTIONS
- Two small black buttons; tapestry needle

GAUGE
- 31 sts and 41 rows = 4" (10 cm) in St st

Sole and Side of Foot

Cast on 12 (14, 16) sts for the heel. Work in St st. At 2¾ (3, 3½)" (7 [8, 9] cm), cast on 27 (30, 33) sts at each side for the side of the foot. 66 (74, 82) sts. At 4 (4½, 5)" (10.5 [11.5, 12.5] cm) bind off.

Top of Foot

Cast on 6 sts. Work in St st. At 1¾" (4.5 cm), cast on 3 (4, 5) sts at each side. 12 (14, 16) sts. At 2¼ (2¾, 3)" (6 [7, 8] cm), dec 1 st at each side every 2 rows 3 times then 1 st on the next row. Bind off.

Strap

Cast on 6 sts. Work in St st. Make a buttonhole on row 3 as follows: k3, YO, k2tog, k1. Work to 2 (2¼, 2¾)" (5 [6, 7] cm) and bind off.

Finishing

Seam the back of the heel by sewing together the edge sts along the side of the foot. Sew the sides to the sole. Set the top in at the opposite side of the heel. Form the loop on the top of the foot as follows: Fold the first 4.5 sts of the top WS together and sew to form a loop. Sew the strap to one side and pass through the loop. Sew a button on the opposite side. Work a second one reversing the strap.

79 – Voyager Booties

Yarn: Sport weight (#2 Fine)
Size: 3 months
Needles: Size US 1 (2.5 mm) and Size US 2 (3 mm)

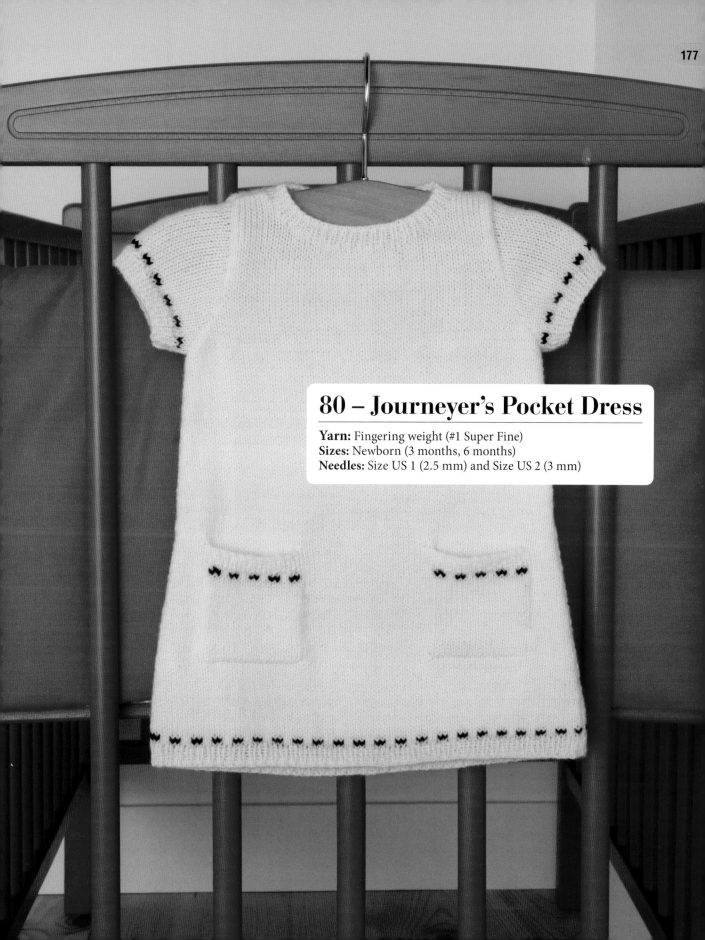

80 – Journeyer's Pocket Dress

Yarn: Fingering weight (#1 Super Fine)
Sizes: Newborn (3 months, 6 months)
Needles: Size US 1 (2.5 mm) and Size US 2 (3 mm)

79 - *Voyager Booties*

SIZE
- 3 months

YARN
- Sport weight (#2 Fine)
  Phildar Lambswool (51% wool, 49% acrylic; 147 yds [134 m]/1.76 oz [50 g]): Noir (C1), 1 skein; Blanc (C2), 1 skein

NEEDLES
- Size US 1 (2.5 mm) and Size US 2 (3 mm)
  Adjust needle size if necessary to obtain the correct gauge.

NOTIONS
- Tapestry needle

GAUGE
- 26 sts and 36 rows = 4" (10 cm) in St st on larger needles

NOTES
- Booties are worked in one piece starting with the back of the heel at the sole

---

Booties

Cast on 11 sts in CC1 on smaller needles. Work 2¾" (7 cm) in garter st then cast on 24 st at each side for the sides. 59 sts. Work 1" (3 cm) in garter st and on the last row work as follows: k 15 sts and put on hold, bind off 10 sts, k 9 sts, bind off 10 sts, k the last 15 sts and put on hold.

Work the top of the foot by working on the center 9 sts in C2. Work 1" (3 cm) in St st. Break the yarn. Working in 1 x 1 ribbing and with C2 work the first 15 sts on hold then the 9 sts of the front of the foot then the last 15 sts. 39 sts. Continue in 1 x 1 ribbing for 2¾" (7 cm) then work 2 rows in C1 and bind off knitwise on the RS or purlwise on the WS. Seam the back reversing the seam on the last 1½" (4 cm). Sew the side to the sole.

80 - *Journeyer's Pocket Dress*

Why would a baby need pockets? Well, why not! Adorn your little one in this adorably chic dress that is worked flat in pieces, then seamed after.

SIZES
- Newborn (3 months, 6 months)

YARN
- Fingering weight (#1 Super Fine)
  Phildar Partner Baby (50% polyamide, 25% wool, 25% acrylic; 117 yds [107 m]/0.88 oz [25 g]): Blanc (MC), 2 (2, 3) skeins
  Phildar Super Baby (70% acrylic, 30% wool; 117 yds [107 m]/0.88 oz [25 g]): Souris (CC), 1 skein

NEEDLES
- Size US 1 (2.5 mm) and Size US 2 (3 mm)
  Adjust needle size if necessary to obtain the correct gauge.

NOTIONS
- Three small white buttons; tapestry needle

GAUGE
- 31 sts and 41 rows = 4" (10 cm) in St st on larger needles

Front

Cast on 83 (89, 95) sts in MC on smaller needles. Work ⅜" (1 cm) of 1 x 1 ribbing then change to St st alternating 2 sts of MC and 2 sts of CC on row 2 only. Dec 1 st at each side every 8 (10, 12) rows 8 times. 67 (73, 79) sts.

At 7 (8¼, 9¾)" (18 [21, 25] cm), shape the armholes. Bind off every 2 rows at each edge every 2 rows: 3 sts 1 time, 2 sts 2 times, and 1 st 4 times. 45 (51, 57) sts. At 8¾ (10¼, 12¼)" (22 [26, 31] cm), bind off the center 9 (11, 13) sts and work each side separately. Bind off at the neckline every 2 rows: 4 sts 1 time, 2 sts 2 times and 1 st 2 times. Work straight for 10¼ (11¾, 13¾)" (26 [30, 35] cm) and bind off all 8 (10, 12) shoulder sts.

Back

Work as for the front to the first row of the armhole dec. Bind off the center st and work each side separately.

At 9¾ (11½, 13¾)" (25 [29, 34] cm), shape the neckline by binding off every 2 rows: 9 (10, 11) sts 1 time and 5 sts 1 time. Continue straight to 10¼ (11¾, 13¾)" (26 [30, 35] cm). Bind off all 8 (10, 12) shoulder sts.

Sleeves

Cast on 46 (52, 58) sts in MC on smaller needles. Work ⅜" (1 cm) of 1 x 1 ribbing then change to larger needles and work in St st. On row 2 only alternate 2 sts of MC and 2 sts of CC.

At ¾ (¾, 1)" (2 [2, 3] cm), bind off at each side every 2 rows: 2 sts 2 times, 1 st 4 times and 2 sts 5 times. Bind off the rest.

Cast on 22 sts in MC on larger needles. Work 2" (5 cm) of St st alternating 2 sts of MC and 2 sts of CC on the next to last row. Work ⅜" (1 cm) 1 x 1 ribbing on smaller needles. Bind off.

Finishing

Sew the shoulders.

Neckline Border: Pick up and k 77 (81, 85) sts in MC on smaller needles, along the neckline. Work ⅜" (1 cm) of 1 x 1 ribbing and bind off.

Back Opening Borders: Pick up and k 32 (35, 38) sts in MC on smaller needles, along a back opening. Work ⅜" (1 cm) of 1 x 1 ribbing and bind off. Work a buttonhole band on the other side making 3, 1 st buttonholes in the middle row, the first 2 sts below the neckline and the rest spaced 10 (12, 13) sts apart. Overlap and sew the 2 borders to the back. Sew on buttons. Seam sleeves to the armhole. Seam the sleeves and sides. Sew the pockets on the lower front.

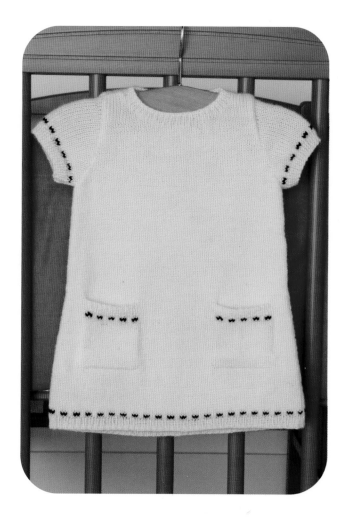

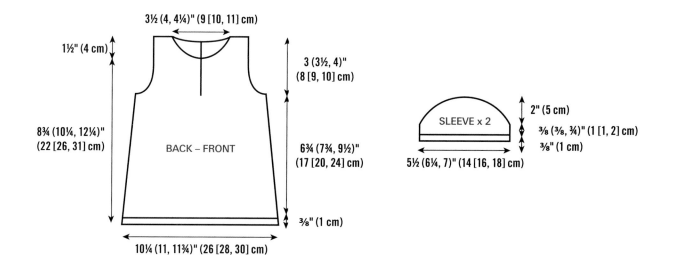

81 – Busy Baby Bonnet

Yarn: Sport weight (#2 Fine)
Sizes: 3 months (6 to 12 months)
Needles: Size US 1 (2.5 mm) and Size US 2 (3 mm)

82 & 83 – Curiosity Cardigan and Sojourner Slacks

Yarn: Sport weight (#2 Fine)
Sizes: 3 months (6 months, 12 months)
Needles: Size US 1 (2.5 mm) and Size US 2 (3 mm)

81 - *Busy Baby Bonnet*

Busy babies need to stay warm too! Whip up this easy-to-pack travel must-have in multiples so you always have backups just in case.

SIZES
- 3 months (6 to 12 months)

YARN
- Sport weight (#2 Fine)
  Phildar Lambswool (51% wool, 49% acrylic; 147 yds [134 m]/1.76 oz [50 g]): Noir (MC) and Blanc (CC), 1 skein each

NEEDLES
- Size US 1 (2.5 mm) and Size US 2 (3 mm)
  Adjust needle size if necessary to obtain the correct gauge.

NOTIONS
- Cable needles; tapestry needle

GAUGE
- 26 sts and 36 rows = 4" (10 cm) in St st on larger needles

Bonnet

Cast on 98 (106) sts in CC on smaller needles. Work ⅜" (1 cm) of 1 x 1 ribbing then change to larger needle and work in St st in MC.

At 4¼ (5)" (11 [13] cm), on the RS, shape the crown as follows: 1 edge stitch,*18 (20) sts, place 3 sts on cable needle and hold in front. K the first st on the cable needle together with the first st on the left needle. Repeat for the next 2 sts on the cable needle. (3 dec) *4 times, 1 edge st.

Repeat these dec (one above the other) every 4 rows 2 more times, then every 2 rows 4 (5) times. Work 8 rows on the remaining 14 (10) sts. Thread the yarn through all the sts and pull tight.

Seam the bonnet.

82 - *Curiosity Cardigan*

Wrap up your little explorer in this cute V-neck cardigan. Complete the outfit by making matching the pants on page 185.

SIZES
- 3 months (6 months, 12 months)

YARN
- Sport weight (#2 Fine)
  Phildar Lambswool (51% wool, 49% acrylic; 147 yds [134 m]/1.76 oz [50 g]): Noir (MC), 2 (3, 3) skeins; Blanc (CC), 1 skein

NEEDLES
- Size US 1 (2.5 mm) and Size US 2 (3 mm)
  Adjust needle size if necessary to obtain the correct gauge.

NOTIONS
- Four small black buttons; tapestry needle

GAUGE
- 26 sts and 36 rows = 4" (10 cm) in St st on larger needles

Back
Cast on 67 (73, 79) sts in CC on smaller needles. Work ⅜" (1 cm) 1 x 1 ribbing. Change to larger needles and work in St st with MC. At 5½ (6¼, 7)" (14 [16, 18] cm), shape the armholes, binding off at each side every 2 rows: 3 sts 1 time, 2 sts 1 time, and 1 st 2 times. 53 (59, 65) sts.
At 9¾ (11, 12¼)" (25 [28, 31] cm), bind of the center 17 (19, 21) sts. Work each side separately. Work 2 rows straight and then bind off 5 sts along the neckline. Work straight to 10¼ (11½, 12½)" (26 [29, 32] cm), bind off the remaining 13 (15, 17) shoulder sts.

Right Front
Cast on 34 (37, 40) sts in CC on smaller needles. Work ⅜" (1 cm) 1 x 1 ribbing. Change to larger needles and work in St st with MC. At 5½ (6¼, 7)" (14 [16, 18] cm), bind off the armhole as for the back at the left edge. 27 (30, 33) sts.
At 6¾ (7½, 8¼)" (17 [19, 21] cm), shape the neckline by dec 1 st at the right edge every 2 rows 14 (15, 16) times. At 10¼ (11½, 12½)" (26 [29, 32] cm), bind off all 13 (15, 17) shoulder sts.

Left Front
Work the same, reversing the shaping.

Sleeves
Cast on 42 (46, 50) sts in CC on smaller needles. Work ⅜" (1 cm) 1 x 1 ribbing. Change to larger needles and work in St st in MC. Inc 1 st at each side: every 4 rows 11 times (every 4 rows 12 times, every alternate 4 and 6 rows 13 times). 64 (70, 76) sts.
At 6 (6¾, 7¾)" (15 [17, 20] cm), bind off at each side every 2 rows: 3 sts 1 time, 2 sts 1 time, and 1 st 2 times. Bind off the rest.

Pockets x 2
Cast on 21 sts in MC on larger needles. Work 2¼" (6 cm) of St st then change to CC and work as follows: k 1 row on RS and then 2 rows of 1 x 1 ribbing. Bind off knitwise on the WS.

82 - *Curiosity Cardigan* (continued)

Finishing

Sew the shoulders. Seam sleeves to the armholes. Seam the sleeves and sides.

Border: Using smaller needles, pick up and k 44 (50, 56) sts in CC on the straight edge of the right front, 33 (36, 39) sts. Along the side of the neckline, 31 (33, 35) sts along the back neckline, then 44 (50, 56) sts along the left front.

Work 2 rows of 1 x 1 ribbing working 4, 1 st buttonholes along the right front with the first 1 st below the start of the neckline, and the rest spaced every 12 (14, 16) sts. Bind off knitwise on the WS.

Attach the pockets to the fronts. Sew on buttons.

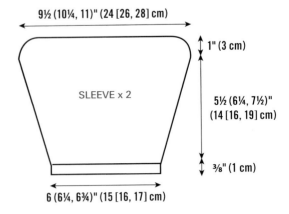

9½ (10¼, 11)" (24 [26, 28] cm)

1" (3 cm)

SLEEVE x 2

5½ (6¼, 7½)" (14 [16, 19] cm)

⅜" (1 cm)

6 (6¼, 6¾)" (15 [16, 17] cm)

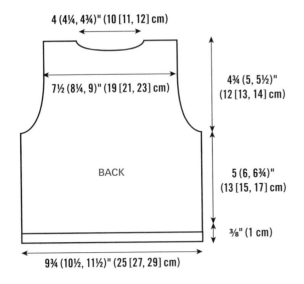

4 (4¼, 4¾)" (10 [11, 12] cm)

7½ (8¼, 9)" (19 [21, 23] cm)

4¾ (5, 5½)" (12 [13, 14] cm)

BACK

5 (6, 6¾)" (13 [15, 17] cm)

⅜" (1 cm)

9¾ (10½, 11½)" (25 [27, 29] cm)

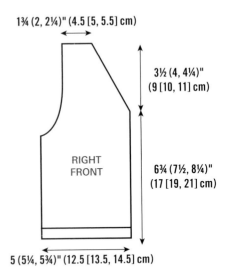

1¾ (2, 2¼)" (4.5 [5, 5.5] cm)

3½ (4, 4¼)" (9 [10, 11] cm)

RIGHT FRONT

6¾ (7½, 8¼)" (17 [19, 21] cm)

5 (5¼, 5¾)" (12.5 [13.5, 14.5] cm)

83 - *Sojourner Slacks*

SIZES
- 3 months (6 months, 12 months)

YARN
- Sport weight (#2 Fine)
  Phildar Lambswool (51% wool, 49% acrylic;
  147 yds [134 m]/1.76 oz [50 g]): Noir (MC), 2
  (3, 3) skeins; Blanc (CC), 1 skein

NEEDLES
- Size US 1 (2.5 mm) and Size US 2 (3 mm)
  *Adjust needle size if necessary to obtain
  the correct gauge.*

NOTIONS
- Elastic thread; tapestry needle

GAUGE
- 26 sts and 36 rows = 4" (10 cm) in St st on
  larger needles

NOTES
- Pants are worked in two pieces and seamed, starting
  at the lower left leg

Back

Cast on 32 (35, 38) sts in CC on larger needles. Work ⅜" (1 cm)
of 1 x 1 ribbing then change to St st working in MC. Inc 1 st at
the right edge as follows: every 6 rows (8 rows, alternate 8 and
10 rows) 9 times. 41 (44, 47) sts. Work to 7 (8¼, 9½)" (18 [21, 24]
cm) and put on hold. Work the right leg reversing the shaping
and then take up the left leg sts. 82 (88, 94) sts. Shape the crotch
by binding off 1 st at either side of the 2 center sts every row 3
times then every 2 rows 3 times. 70 (76, 82) sts.
At 13 (14½, 16½)" (33 [37, 42] cm), for the waist, work 1" (3 cm)
of 1 x 1 ribbing on smaller needles, then bind off.

Front

Work as for the back.

Finishing

Seam back and front along the side and inside leg. Thread
several rows of elastic under the waist ribbing.

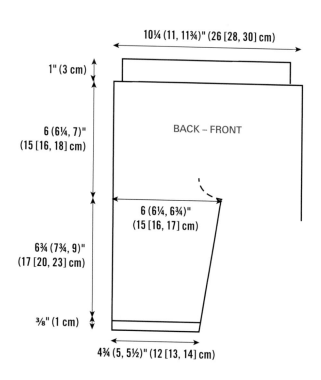

10¼ (11, 11¾)" (26 [28, 30] cm)

1" (3 cm)

6 (6¼, 7)"
(15 [16, 18] cm)

BACK – FRONT

6 (6¼, 6¾)"
(15 [16, 17] cm)

6¾ (7¾, 9)"
(17 [20, 23] cm)

⅜" (1 cm)

4¾ (5, 5½)" (12 [13, 14] cm)

Floral and Fun

84 – Carnation Cap

Yarn: DK weight (#3 Light)
Sizes: Newborn to 3 months (6 months)
Needles: Size US 4 (3.5 mm)

85 – Chrysanthemum Cardigan

Yarn: DK weight (#3 Light)
Sizes: Newborn (3 months, 6 months)
Needles: Size US 2 (3 mm) and Size US 4 (3.5 mm)

86 – Pretty Picot Pants

Yarn: DK weight (#3 Light)
Sizes: Newborn (3 months, 6 months)
Needles: Size US 2 (3 mm) and Size US 4 (3.5 mm)

87 – Summery Slip-Ons

Yarn: DK weight (#3 Light)
Sizes: Newborn to 3 months (6 months)
Needles: Size US 2 (3 mm)

84 - *Carnation Cap*

Fickle spring weather makes dressing your baby a challenge. A cute cotton cap like this one is excellent for keeping ears warm in slightly cooler temps while also being light enough to wear on warmer days.

SIZES
- Newborn to 3 months (6 months)

YARN
- DK weight (#3 Light)
  Phildar Phil Cotton 4 (100% cotton; 93 yds [85 m]/1.76 oz [50 g]): Craie (MC), Soleil (CC1), Rouge (CC2), Œillet (CC3), 1 skein each

NEEDLES
- Size US 4 (3.5 mm)
  Adjust needle size if necessary to obtain the correct gauge.

NOTIONS
- Size US C-2 (2.75 mm) crochet hook; cable needle; tapestry needle

GAUGE
- 20 sts and 28 rows = 4" (10 cm) in St st

SPECIAL STITCHES
- **Single crochet:** sc
- **Double crochet:** dc
- **Chain stitch (crochet):** ch st
- **Crochet Flowers:** Make a loop then *ch 2, dc, ch 2, sc in the same loop *5 times
- **Crochet Picot:** *sl 2, ch 3, 1 sl st in the first ch *

Bonnet
Cast on 74 (78) sts with MC and work in St st. At 2¾ (3½)" (7 [9] cm), work the crown shaping as follows: *sl the next 3 sts to a cable needle and hold in back. K the first st on the left needle together with first st on the cable needle. Repeat for the next 2 sts. Work 12 (13) sts *4 times, 1 edge stitch. Repeat this dec rows stacking the dec on top of each other after 4 rows then after every 2 rows 3 (4) times. Draw the yarn through the remaining 14 (6) sts and pull tight. Secure the end.
Work a row of sc around the edge then work a row of picot. Seam closed. Make 1 flower each in CC1. CC2, CC3 and sew in place.

85 - *Chrysanthemum Cardigan*

Cute crochet flowers are the perfect addition to this light cotton cardi. Stretchy ribbing across the chest also means added room for your baby to grow.

SIZES
- Newborn (3 months, 6 months)

YARN
- DK weight (#3 Light)
  Phildar Phil Cotton 4 (100% cotton; 93 yds [85 m]/1.76 oz [50 g]): Craie (MC), Soleil (CC1), Rouge (CC2), Œillet (CC3), 1 skein each

NEEDLES
- Size US 4 (3.5 mm)
  Adjust needle size if necessary to obtain the correct gauge.

NOTIONS
- Size US C-2 (2.75 mm) crochet hook; three garment snaps; tapestry needle

GAUGE
- 20 sts and 28 rows = 4" (10 cm) in St st

SPECIAL STITCHES
- **Single crochet:** sc
- **Double crochet:** dc
- **Chain stitch (crochet):** ch st
- **Crochet Flowers:** make a loop then *ch 2, dc, ch 2, ch 1 in the loop *5 times
- **Crochet Picot:** *sl 2, ch3, 1 sl st in first ch *

Back

Cast on 47 (51, 55) sts in MC. Work in St st. At 4¼ (4¾, 5)" (11 [12, 13] cm), change to 2 x 1 ribbing starting with: p 2 (p 1, k 1). At 4¾ (5½, 6¼)" (12 [14, 16] cm), shape the armholes, binding off at each side every 2 rows: 2 sts 2 times then 1 st 2 times. 35 (39, 43) sts.
At 8¼ (9½, 10½)" (21 [24, 27] cm), bind off the center 9 (11, 13) sts and work each side separately. Work 2 rows then bind off 5 sts at the neckline. Continue straight to 8¾ (9¾, 11)" (22 [25, 28] cm). Bind off 8 (9, 10) shoulder sts.

Right Front

Cast on 22 (24, 26) sts in MC. Work in St st. At 4¼ (4¾, 5)" (11 [12, 13] cm) change to 2 x 1 ribbing starting with p1 (p2, k1). At 4¾ (5½, 6¼)" (12 [14, 16] cm), bind off along the left edge for the armhole as for the back. 16 (18, 20) sts.
At 7½ (8¾, 9¾)" (19 [22, 25] cm) bind off along the right edge to shape the neckline every other row: 3 (4, 5) sts 1 time, 2 sts 1 time, 1 st 3 times. Work to 8¾ (9¾, 11)" (22 [25, 28] cm) and bind off all 8 (9, 10) shoulder sts.

Left Front

Work the same, reversing the shaping.

Sleeves

Cast on 28 (30, 32) sts, work in St st. Inc 1 st at each side as follows: every 4 rows 6 times (every 5 rows 7 times, every 5 rows 8 times). 40 (44, 48) sts.
At 4 (5½, 6¼)" (10 [14, 16] cm), bind off at each side every 2 rows 1 st 2 times and 2 sts 2 times. Bind off the rest.

Finishing

Button Bands: Pick up and k 32 (38, 44) sts along each front. Work ¾" (2 cm) of St st and bind off. Sew the shoulders. With crochet hook, work 1 row of sc at the edge of each front and the neckline.
Seam sleeves to the armhole. Seam the sleeves and sides. Work a row of sc then a row of crochet picots around the bottom of the cardigan, the wrists and the neckline. Crochet 1 flower in each CC1, CC2, and CC3 and sew on to the button band spaced every ⅜ (¾, 1)" (1 [2, 3] cm). Sew snaps under the flowers.

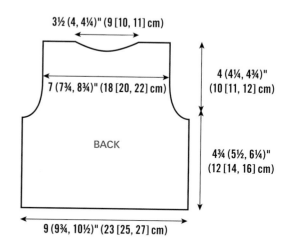

3½ (4, 4¼)" (9 [10, 11] cm)

7 (7¾, 8¾)" (18 [20, 22] cm)

4 (4¼, 4¾)" (10 [11, 12] cm)

BACK

4¾ (5½, 6¼)" (12 [14, 16] cm)

9 (9¾, 10½)" (23 [25, 27] cm)

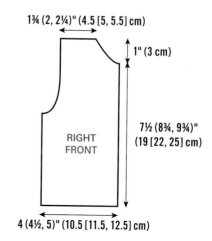

1¾ (2, 2¼)" (4.5 [5, 5.5] cm)

1" (3 cm)

RIGHT FRONT

7½ (8¾, 9¾)" (19 [22, 25] cm)

4 (4½, 5)" (10.5 [11.5, 12.5] cm)

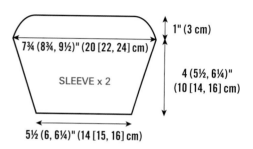

1" (3 cm)

7¾ (8¾, 9½)" (20 [22, 24] cm)

SLEEVE x 2

4 (5½, 6¼)" (10 [14, 16] cm)

5½ (6, 6¼)" (14 [15, 16] cm)

86 - *Pretty Picot Pants*

Cotton pants are an ideal choice when dressing your baby for warmer days. Make these pants in various springtime colors, or omit the picot edging for a more neutral look.

SIZES
- Newborn (3 months, 6 months)

YARN
- DK weight (#3 Light)
  Phildar Phil Cotton 4 (100% cotton; 93 yds [85 m]/1.76 oz [50 g]): Craie, 2 (3, 4) skeins

NEEDLES
- Size US 2 (3 mm) and Size US 4 (3.5 mm)
  Adjust needle size if necessary to obtain the correct gauge.

NOTIONS
- Size US C-2 (2.75 mm) crochet hook; elastic thread; tapestry needle

GAUGE
- 20 sts and 28 rows = 4" (10 cm) in St st on larger needles

SPECIAL STITCHES
- **Single crochet:** sc
- **Double crochet:** dc
- **Chain stitch (crochet):** ch st
- **Crochet Picot:** *sl 2, ch3, 1 sl st in first ch *

Back
Cast on 22 (24, 26) sts on larger needles. Work in St st inc 1 st at the right edge every 4 (5, 6) rows 8 times. Work to 5 (6¼, 7½)" (13 [16, 19] cm) then put the 30 (32, 34) sts on hold. Work the left leg sts on hold and continue on the 60 (64, 68) sts. Shape the crotch by dec 1 st on either side of the center 2 sts every row 2 times then every 2 rows 2 times. 52 (56, 60) sts.
At 10½ (12½, 14½)" (27 [32, 37] cm), change to smaller needles. Work 1" (3 cm) of 1 x 1 ribbing and bind off.

Front
Work as for the back.

Finishing
Sew the sides. Work a row of sc and a row of crochet picots along the bottom of the legs. Sew the leg seams. Thread several rows of elastic thread under the waist ribbing.

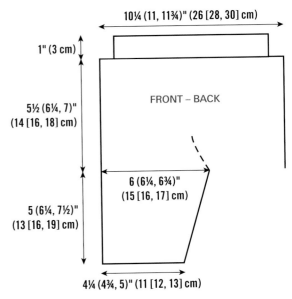

10¼ (11, 11¾)" (26 [28, 30] cm)

1" (3 cm)

FRONT – BACK

5½ (6¼, 7)" (14 [16, 18] cm)

6 (6¼, 6¾)" (15 [16, 17] cm)

5 (6¼, 7½)" (13 [16, 19] cm)

4¼ (4¾, 5)" (11 [12, 13] cm)

87 - *Summery Slip-Ons*

What's summer without a cute pair of strappy slip-ons? Garter stitch gives these shoes a fun texture, while the added crocheted flowers provide a pop of color perfect for the season.

SIZES
- Newborn to 3 months (6 months)

YARN
- DK weight (#3 Light)
  Phildar Phil Cotton 4 (100% cotton; 93 yds [85 m]/1.76 oz [50 g]): Craie (MC), Rouge (CC1), Œillet (CC2), 1 skein each

NEEDLES
- Size US 4 (3.5 mm)
  Adjust needle size if necessary to obtain the correct gauge.

NOTIONS
- Size US C-2 (2.75 mm) crochet hook; tapestry needle

GAUGE
- 23 sts and 56 rows = 4" (10 cm) in garter st

SPECIAL STITCHES
- **Single crochet:** sc
- **Double crochet:** dc
- **Chain stitch (crochet):** ch st
- **Crochet Flowers:** make a loop and work: *ch 2, dc, ch2, sl 1 st in the loop *5 times

Sole
Cast on 6 (8) sts. Work in garter st and inc 1 st at each side every 2 rows 3 times. 12 (14) sts. At 2¾ (3)" (7 [8] cm), dec 1 st at each side every 2 rows 3 times. Bind off.

Side of Foot
Cast on 46 (54) sts. Work 11 rows of garter st and bind off.

Top of Foot
Cast on 3 sts. On row 20 inc at each side every 2 rows: 1 st 2 times and 2 sts 1 time (1 st 2 times and 3 sts 1 time). 11 (13) sts. At 3 (3¼)" (8 [8.5] cm), dec 1 st at each side every 2 rows 3 times. Bind off the rest.

Strap
Cast on 15(18) sts. Work 4 rows in garter st and bind off.

Finishing
Seam the side closed at the heel and seam to the sole. Seam the top to the sides. Fold the first 20 rows in half WS together and sew to form a loop. Pass the strap through the loop and sew to each side.
Crochet a flower in CC1 and CC2. Sew a flower on each top.

Index

A

abbreviations, 8

animals: bears, 85, 89, 167, 169–170; bunnies, 12, 36–37; cats, 12, 14, 68, 70; mice 12, 16, 137–139, 140–141, 149, 154–155

B

blankets, 13 ,18, 43, 48, 148, 150

blanket stitch, 94, 99

bonnets, 21, 25, 33, 31, 82, 86, 93, 99, 112, 115, 124, 126, 145, 146, 181, 182, 187, 188

booties, 21, 24, 35, 35, 41, 42, 47, 61, 65, 66, 101, 104, 131, 135, 148, 153, 162, 164, 173, 175, 176, 178, 187, 191

C

caps, 21, 25, 33, 31, 82, 86, 93, 99, 112, 115, 124, 126, 145, 146, 181, 182, 187, 188

coats, 27, 28–29, 51–53, 92, 94–97, 109, 110–111, 125, 128–129, 166, 168–169

D

dresses, 76, 78–79, 163, 165, 177, 178–179

E

edge stitch, 8

F

frog "button" embellishment, 129

G

garter stitch, 8

gauge, 8

H

hats, 21, 25, 33, 31, 82, 86, 93, 99, 112, 115, 124, 126, 145, 146, 181, 182, 187, 187, 188

J

jackets, 27, 28–29, 51–53, 92, 94–97, 109, 110–111, 125, 128–129, 166, 168–169

jumpsuit, 42, 44–46

L

leggings 76, 80–81, 130, 133

M

mittens, 21, 25, 82, 86, 93, 99

O

1 x 1 ribbing, 8

overalls, 30, 32–33

P

pants, 20, 23–24, 30, 32–33, 34, 40, 60, 64, 68, 74, 76, 80–81, 84, 88–89, 101, 107, 113, 118, 125, 127, 130, 133, 157, 161, 181, 185, 187, 190

R

reverse stockinette stitch, 8

romper, 131, 134

row, 8

S

sacks, 54, 55, 56–57, 58–59, 85, 90–91, 120, 122–123

safety, 9

scarf 93, 98

shawl, 13, 18

sizes, choosing, 8

slip stitch, 8

slip 1 knit 1 pass slipped stitch over (skp), 8

slippers, 35, 41, 61, 66, 131, 135, 162, 164

socks, 68, 75, 112, 114

stockinette stitch (St st), 8

stop work, where to 9

strands, working several, 8

sweaters, 22, 60, 61, 62–63, 66–67, 68, 72–73, 84, 86–87, 100, 101, 102–103, 105–106, 113, 116–117, 130, 132, 136–139, 145, 146–147, 148, 151–152, 171, 172, 174–175, 181, 183–184, 187, 188–189

T

take up, 8

tops, 20, 22–23, 34, 38–39, 60, 61, 62–63, 66–67, 68, 76, 78–79, 84, 86–87, 100, 101, 102–103, 105–106, 113, 116–117, 130, 132, 136–139, 142–143, 145, 146–147, 148, 151–152, 157, 158–160, 171, 172, 174–175, 183–184, 187, 188–189

2 x 1 ribbing, 8

2 x 2 ribbing, 8

W

washing hand knits, 9

Y

yarn over (yo), 8